HANDS ON
RIGID HEDDLE
WEAVING

Betty Linn Davenport

Illustrations by Ann Sabin

INTERWEAVE.
interweave.com

Photography by Joe Coca
Cover by Signorella Graphic Arts

Interweave
A division of F+W Media, Inc.
4868 Innovation Drive
Fort Collins, CO   80525   USA

Manufactured in Canada by Friesens

Library of Congress Cataloging-in-Publication Data
Davenport, Betty Linn, 1939–
    Hands on rigid heddle weaving.
    Bibliography: p.
    1. Hand weaving.   I. Davenport, Betty Linn, 1939–
    II. Title   III. Rigid heddle weaving.
  TT848.D29   1987   746.1'45   86-83426
  ISBN 978-0-934026-25-3 (pbk.)

CONTENTS

Introduction

There is a quiet pleasure in knowing that you made the scarf you're wearing, the towel by the sink, or the decorative piece in your entryway. The act of weaving, watching the fabric come into existence as the yarn goes back and forth, is almost magical.

The rigid heddle loom offers a simple and affordable way to produce many kinds of beautiful fabrics, from table mats and clothing to blankets and many things in between. The large, harness-type looms that are so obvious in museums and in weaving shops are much more expensive and not necessarily more flexible, although they can produce certain types of fabrics more efficiently. The rigid heddle is a loom to learn on, and a loom to continue with. You may find that other looms have entered your life after your experience with the rigid heddle, or other looms may have come first. In either case, this is a loom to have fun with and a loom for serious work—and you don't have to limit yourself to one or the other!

Weaving is all around you. Your blue jeans, bed sheets, window screens, dish towels—most of the fabrics that you wear, sleep on, and otherwise surround yourself with in your daily life are woven. And even if you've never owned a loom or taken a weaving class, chances are good that you've experienced the act of weaving at one time or other. Maybe you made potholders on a ''jersey-loop'' loom, or wove paper place mats in grade school. Maybe you wove a basket in Girl Scouts, or endured weaving round and round on a paper plate.

Anyone can weave, and with any fibrous material—yarn, reeds, strips of paper or cloth. The possibilities are endless. Just lay out some parallel fibers and then take another strand of fiber and go over-under-over-under the original parallel set. That's weaving.

Of course, weaving can get a lot more complex than that. After you've woven something simple, you begin to think. A tool which would hold the parallel strands taut and steady would help. So would a way to lift every other thread so the weaving strand could slip quickly on its way. There has to be a neat trick for pushing the weaving thread into place so there's room to weave the next row. And how about making something *long* or *wide?*

Looms were invented to make all these weaving steps easier. Looms come in all sizes and shapes, and have been developed all over the world in different cultures. All looms keep that first set of parallel strands, called the **warp,** orderly and under enough tension to be easy to work with.

Most, but not all, looms also make it easy to raise or lower some of the threads so that the weaving thread, called the **weft,** can slide through quickly. If you lift every other thread, the opening between the lifted and unlifted threads is called a **shed.** You can poke the weft through this opening, instead of working it over and under one warp thread at a time. Lowering those threads and lifting the alternate threads makes a new shed.

To make a piece of cloth which is longer than your loom, you need to be able to make long warp threads and wind them up at the back of the loom to keep them orderly and out of the way until you need them. You also need to be able to wind up and store the woven cloth at the front of the loom until you have finished weaving it. Some looms make this possible.

Finally, the looms we use today usually have a way to press the weft threads into place.

And that brings us to the rigid heddle loom, which is this book's topic. **The rigid heddle loom combines all these conveniences with a frame that is still lightweight and inexpensive.**

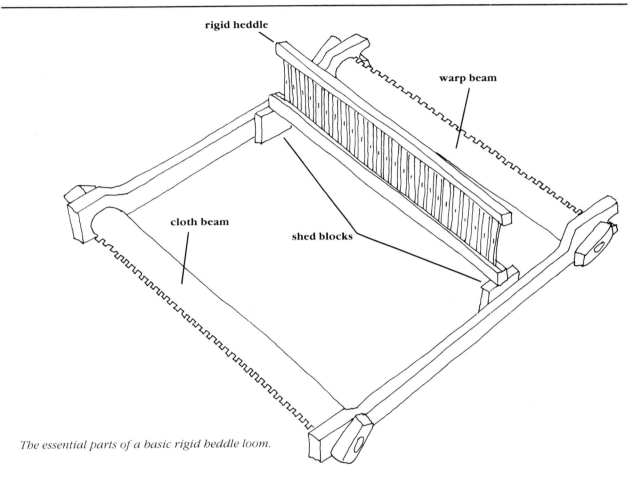

The essential parts of a basic rigid heddle loom.

So how does it work? At back of the loom the unwoven warp is stored on a **warp beam** which can be turned to unroll the warp as needed. From this warp beam at the back, the threads then go forward through the slots and holes of the **rigid heddle**—the working part of the loom.

The rigid heddle is a series of plastic bars set vertically into a frame. Each bar has a **hole** in it; the spaces between the bars are called **slots.** Warp yarns are threaded alternately through the holes and the slots. When you lift the heddle, the warps threaded through the holes rise while those in the slots stay where they are. If you push the heddle down, the warps in the holes sink below the warps in the slots, which still stay put. In either case, the opening between the two sets of warps forms a shed through which the weft can travel. On the sides of the loom are **shed blocks,** to hold the heddle in the up position or the down position as you slide the weft through the shed.

The weaving actually takes place in the shed in front of the heddle, where the weft threads go through between the raised and lowered warp threads. So the woven cloth is formed between the heddle and the front of the loom. As weaving proceeds, new warp is rolled off the warp beam. The woven cloth is stored on another rotating beam, the **cloth beam,** at the front of the loom.

How to Choose a
Rigid Heddle Loom

Think about the different situations in which you will use the loom. Do you want to take it on trips? Do you have table or floor space to leave it set up? If not, where will you store it? If your loom is convenient, you will enjoy weaving often.

If you have the opportunity, try out different looms before you buy. At least sit down with the loom in weaving position. Check the depth of the loom—most are 20 inches (50 cm) from front to back, and some are longer. Can you easily reach the back beam and can you reach your tools and yarn on the table?

Most rigid heddle looms range in width from 14 to 35 inches (35 to 89 cm), although a few are even larger. Looms made by the various manufacturers are designed to be supported or used in different ways, and each loom has a particular combination of features.

Weaving position

Because comfort is primary, let's start by considering the position in which you'll weave. Rigid heddle looms are made for use in three different basic positions. Although some modifications are possible, once you have chosen your loom, you have chosen your weaving position. The basic choices for where your loom will be placed are:

On top of a table. Some rigid heddle looms are designed to be placed on top of a table. These will need to be clamped to the table so they won't move around whenever the heddle is shifted. Standard tables are often uncomfortably high for long weaving sessions, so you can either find a low table or adapt the loom to rest against the table edge or to fit a floor stand.

Supported between your body and a table edge. You sit in a chair with the loom wedged between your body and the table edge. Some looms are notched at the back to fit over a table edge. If the table edge is too thick for the notch, a 1 × 4″ board may be clamped to the table, extending from the edge a little, to make a lip for the notched end to rest against. If the loom doesn't have notches, it can be rested with the shed blocks against the table; this holds the loom in place almost as firmly.

Attached to a stand. Many manufacturers have designed floor stands to which their looms can be attached. A loom on a floor stand is very comfortable to work at, although a stand may cost as much as the loom itself. Most floor stands can be adjusted for height and have foot rests which help stabilize the loom. Some also fold up for storage with the loom attached. Some stands can be easily removed, so the loom can be used in another location. A stand is especially nice if you have enough space to leave the loom set up or if you do not have a suitable table to use as a support. Looms wider than 24 inches (60 cm) will be easier to handle on a stand.

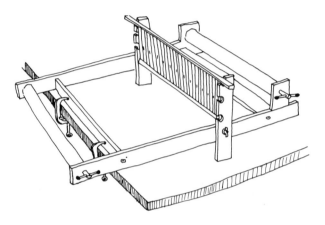

A table-top loom designed to be clamped in place; this loom also has brackets, rather than shed blocks, to support the rigid heddle.

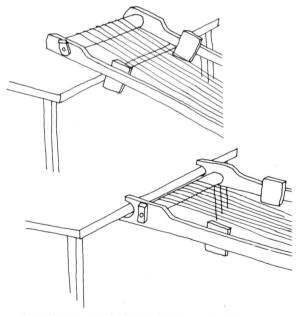

Some looms can be braced between your body and a table; the model above uses the shed blocks as braces and the model below has special notches at the loom's back.

A loom on a stand requires some floor space, but offers other advantages.

Weight and portability

Wider looms and looms with stands are heavier than narrow looms that rest on or against a table. They also take more floor space—but you may be happy to give up floor space in exchange for freeing the dining room table. Wider looms allow you to weave wider fabrics and may accommodate longer warps.

Lightweight looms, on the other hand, are very portable. If your work space is limited, this loom is the answer: all you need is a chair and a table edge. When this loom is not being used, it can be leaned against a wall or stored in a closet or behind a door. Many lightweight looms can be disassembled with a weaving in place, rolled up, and packed in a suitcase. Take your weaving with you! As the most inexpensive type of rigid heddle loom, the lightweight design is ideal for the beginner as well as for the experienced weaver who needs a portable loom.

Length of warp

How long a piece you can weave on the loom may make a difference to you, although most rigid heddle looms can handle a reasonable length of weaving. The maximum length of warp that can be wound onto a loom's back beam depends on its design and varies between 1 and 15 yards (1 and 13.7 m), although most hold between 4½ and 10 yards (4 and 9 m).

There are two basic arrangements by which the warp can travel from the back beam to the front beam as it is made into cloth. One type of loom simply has the warp and cloth beams; the warp winds off the back beam, through the heddles, and onto the front beam. As the warp winds onto the back beam, it makes a thick roll that, on very long warps, might interfere with making a good shed.

If the warp goes directly from beam to beam, the total feasible warp length is between 3 and 4½ yards (2.7 and 4 m), depending on the thickness of the yarn. Four yards is enough for most projects, including garments.

The other type of loom includes cross-braces, one above each of the two beams. The warp winds off the back (warp) beam, over the back brace, through the heddles, over the front brace, and onto the front (cloth) beam. These braces control the level of the warp. As much warp can be wound onto the beams as there is space for it to build up. The level of the warp does not change as it rolls from back to front. Some looms of this design can handle up to 15 yards (13.7 m). Check the braces to be sure they won't bend under the stress of a tight warp. Some looms of the first type have cross-braces which provide only stability and do not affect the level of the warp; cross-braces on this second type of loom will be above the warp and cloth beams and will keep the warp level constant.

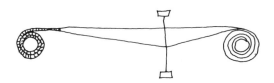

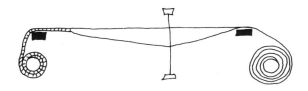

Above: the warp travels directly from beam to beam. Below: cross-braces on the loom may allow more warp length to be wound around the warp and cloth beams without affecting the level of the warp as it passes through the heddle.

Tensioning device

The warp and cloth beams of the looms you are considering will be equipped with tensioning devices to keep the beams from rotating when you don't want them to. Some looms are tensioned by a simple wooden knob or wing-nut which puts pressure on the ends of the beams when it is tightened. The wing-nuts should be large enough that you can get a good grip on them or they won't tighten well enough to hold the warp tension. Others have a **ratchet**—a tooth-edged part—which can be held steady by a **dog** or **pawl.**

Some warp and cloth beams have plastic "teeth," or pegs, to which the ends of the warp yarns are attached. Others have dowel rods, which are in turn attached to the beams with cords. Either way of attaching the warp ends to the beam is satisfactory, and both will be explained.

Toothed beams, above, and dowel rods with extension cords, below, work equally well when it comes time to secure your warp to the beams. They do require slightly different techniques.

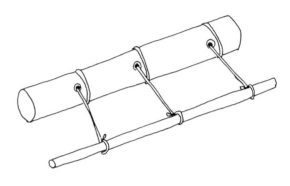

A ratchet and pawl.

A wing-nut works on the same principle as a threaded knob.

Rigid heddles can be supported by shed blocks, left, or brackets, right.

Shed positions

Another thing you will want to consider is the loom's method of holding the heddle in the two shed positions—up and down. Some looms have a simple block on the side of the loom. The heddle sits on the block for the up shed, and hooks under it in the down shed. On other looms, the heddle hangs from a holder. Advanced rigid heddle techniques that use two or more heddles can only be done on a loom with simple blocks, since there must be room to make a shed with two heddles together. You have to be able to move the heddles in front of or behind the shed block, and you can't do that if the heddle hangs from a bracket. The good news is that you will be able to do nearly all of the techniques presented in this book on either type of loom.

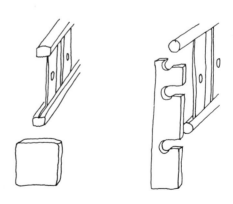

The chart of rigid heddle looms here will help you choose a loom that will meet your needs. These manufactureres are well established and known for quality products. The specifications are current as we go to press, but improvements and modifications occur. Your best final guides will be the looms themselves, supplemented by the latest catalogs from the manufacturers.

Chart of Rigid Heddle Looms

Manufacturer	Model	Width(s)	Standard heddle	Additional heddles available	Accommodates multiple heddles	Maximum warp length	Warp attached by	Loom support system	Floor stand available	Wood used for loom
Beka[1] (United States)	SG	14" (35 cm) 20" (50 cm) 24" (60 cm)	10/" (40/10)	8/" (32/10) 10/" (40/10) 12/" (48/10)	yes	4.5 yd (4 m)	teeth	table edge	yes, extra	cherry
	RL	24" (60 cm) 32" (80 cm)	Same as SG	Same as SG	yes	15 yd (14 m)	teeth	floor stand	included	cherry
Schacht (United States)		20" (50 cm) 25" (62.5 cm) 35" (89 cm)	8/" (32/10)	8/" (32/10) 10/" (40/10) 12/" (48/10)	yes	10 yd (9 m)	dowel	table surface or edge	yes, extra	maple
LeClerc (Canada)		24" (60 cm)	6/" (24/10)	8/" (32/10) 10/" (40/10) 12/" (48/10)	no	3 yd (2.7 m)	dowel	table surface	no	hardwood
Ashford (New Zealand)		40 cm (16") 60 cm (24")	34/10 (8.5/")	20/10 (5/") 40/10 (10/")	no	3 yd (2.7 m)	dowel	table edge (new) table surface (old)	no	silver beech
Glimakra[2] (Sweden)		35 cm (13.5") 46 cm (18") 70 cm (27")	30/10 (8/") 40/10 (10") 50/10 (12/")	30/10 (8/") 40/10 (10/") 50/10 (12/")	yes	15 yd (14 m)	dowel	table surface or edge	yes, extra	birch
Kircher (West Germany)	SW	30 cm (12") 40 cm (16") 50 cm (20")	40/10 (10/")	20/10 (5/") 30/10 (7.5/") 60/10 (15/")	yes	5 m (5.5 yd)	teeth	table edge	no	hardwood
	W	60 cm (24") 80 cm (31.5") 100 cm (39.5")	40/10 (10/")	Same as SW	yes	10 m (11 yd)	teeth	table edge or floor stand	yes, extra	hardwood
Lervad[3] (Denmark)	No. 15	40 cm (16") 60 cm (24")	40/10 (10/")	24/10 (6/") 36/10 (8/") 45/10 (11.5/") 50/10 (12.5/") 60/10 (15/") 80/10 (20/")	no	6 m (6.5 yd)	dowel	table surface	no	beech
	No. 11	40 cm (16") 60 cm (24") 80 cm (31.5") 100 cm (39.5")	40/10 (10/")	Same as No. 15	no	10 m (11 yd)	dowel	floor stand	included	beech

[1]The 14" Beka SG is made of maple, instead of cherry, and cannot be used with a floor stand. The Beka RL series can be obtained with a double back beam, for use in some advanced rigid heddle techniques beyond the scope of this book. [2]The Glimakra loom comes with pegs that convert the back of the loom itself into a warping board. [3]Lervad heddles (with the exception of the 40/10) are made of metal, which allows them to produce finer setts.

A First Project

For your first experience in weaving, I'm presenting a sample project for a table runner or pillow. It includes techniques that will give you a firm foundation for future projects: warping your loom, making sheds, beating the weft in place, and so forth. You will be able to concentrate on basic weaving skills because some of the decisions, such as what yarn to use and how long a warp to put on your loom, have been made for you.

Getting Ready

Gathering tools

You'll need a rigid heddle loom, of course, with one heddle and all the equipment which came with it. You probably have either an 8-dent (32 dents/10 cm) or a 10-dent (40 dents/10 cm) heddle, since these are most often supplied with looms. To find out which your loom has, look for a number stamped on the heddle or count the number of holes *and* slots in one inch of the heddle.[1]

Several other pieces of equipment will make weaving go more smoothly. Before you begin, gather the following or their substitutes:

Crochet hook: You will use this to pull the warp threads through the heddle. Use a size 8 steel hook for either the 8-dent (32/10) or 10-dent (40/10) heddle. Sometimes you can poke the yarns through with your fingers; it's slower, but if it's midnight and you want to get going don't let the lack of a crochet hook hold you back.

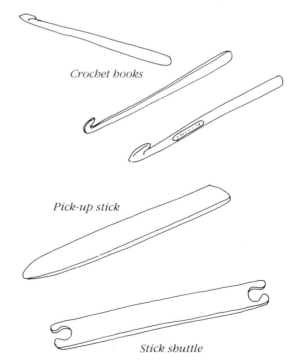

Crochet hooks

Pick-up stick

Stick shuttle

[1]Metric heddles are designated by the number of holes and slots in 10 centimeters. To convert a metric designation to dents per inch, divide the first number by four. A metric 40/10 heddle is the equivalent of a 10-dent heddle, and a 32/10 is an 8-dent heddle.

Pick-up stick or shed stick: This is a flat wooden stick with one rounded end, used to pick up warp threads for some kinds of pattern weaving. You'll need a pick-up stick for the first project. You can buy a stick or make one from flat molding stock from the lumberyard; sand all the edges smooth so they won't snag the yarn.

Stick shuttles: These are flat wooden sticks, notched at both ends. They hold the weft yarn and carry it through the sheds. The yarn is wound lengthwise onto the shuttle between the notches. Stick shuttles are easiest to use if they are a little longer than the warp is wide. For the first project, the warp will be 14 inches (35.5 cm) wide; you will need four stick shuttles about 16 inches (38 cm) long. You can make these but they're cheap enough that you may not want to.

Two large kraft-paper grocery bags or other heavy brown paper
Strip of cardboard or paper, 2" × 16"
Scissors
Measuring tape
Tapestry needle (large, blunt needle)
Ballpoint pen
Strong yarn or string in a color which contrasts with your warp

Other "nice but not necessary" tools, along with their substitutes, include:

Ball winder to wind the yarn into balls quickly and easily.

Umbrella swift to hold the skeins of yarn while you wind them into balls; instead, you can have another person hold the skein, drop the skein over the back of a straight chair, or, if you're agile enough, you can use your own knees to hold the skein open while you wind a ball.

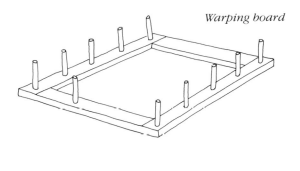

Warping board

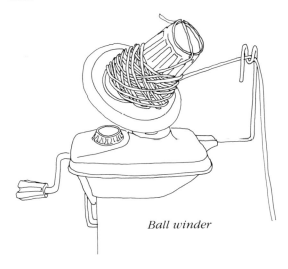

Ball winder

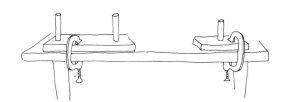

Warping pegs

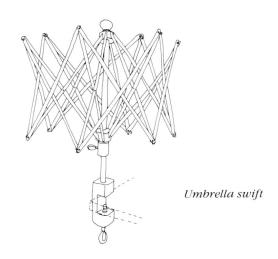

Umbrella swift

Warping tools: There are several ways to measure the warp yarns before you put them on the loom. If you have or can borrow a *warping board,* use it. If not, a set of *warping pegs* will do the job. This is a set of two blocks which you clamp to a table as far apart as you want your warp to be long. As you wind the warp, you must walk back and forth, but the pegs are inexpensive and work well. You can also attach three C-clamps to a table or counter upside down and wind the warp around their shafts.

Preparations

Marking the heddle. If you mark your heddle—and also your warp and cloth beams—you'll always know where the center of your loom is, and you won't have to haul out a measuring tape each time you want to put a warp on your loom. Looms work best if the warps are centered. Mark your loom once and forever reap the benefits.

First, use the measuring tape to find the center of the heddle. Measure from one edge of the plastic bars to the other. With a ballpoint pen, mark the wooden frame in line with the center slot and then mark every inch (or in metric, every 2 cm) out to the edges. Label each mark, starting in the center with 0 and numbering out to the edges. Do the same on the front and back beams if they have notches or teeth to which the warp will be attached. If you have dowel rods you will be able to slide the warps until they are straight, so marking is optional.

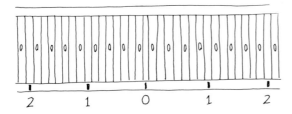

Preparing paper inserts. You'll hear a lot about *tension* as we go along, because it's so important, and while tension problems can be cured, they're simpler to prevent. For trouble-free weaving, it's important to wind the layers of warp evenly onto the beam, so they'll come *off* the beam evenly. Sheets of heavy paper can be wound with the warp to separate each layer and to keep the warp from building up more thickly in some places than others.

Large grocery bags of heavy brown paper work well. Open the bag and trim the paper to fit the full width of the back beam of your loom. The paper must be wider than the warp so that the yarns at the edges don't fall off the paper. If you cut the paper as wide as the back beam you will be ready for any project. The paper may be easier to handle if you cut it into two lengths. Roll each sheet into a tube to give it a curl. These sheets can be used many times for different projects.

INSTRUCTIONS for the first project are presented in short form on pages 14-15. The text in the rest of this chapter gives you the background and step by step procedures for weaving the project.

Choosing yarns

Wool weaving yarns are easy to work with and quite forgiving for a first project. Your choice of yarn depends on the size of heddle that came with your loom. Some well-known brands of yarn that are suitable for either a 10-dent or an 8-dent heddle are listed below. Avoid using wool or acrylic knitting worsteds until you have more experience; they are much softer and stretchier than weaving yarns and can present unnecessary problems. Many other knitting yarns work well in weaving, though.

A rule-of-thumb technique for finding the right size yarn involves wrapping the yarn around a ruler and counting the turns per inch. Push the strands together so they are touching but not overlapping. For a balanced weave structure, with the same number of warps and wefts per inch, the yarn should have twice as many turns in 1 inch (2.5 cm) as your heddle has dents in 1 inch (2.5 cm). In other words, if your heddle has 10 dents per inch, look for yarns that have 20 turns in an inch. For an 8-dent heddle, look for yarns that wrap 16 turns per inch.

If you want to work in colors of your own choice, select three colors that you like or that harmonize with the furnishings in your house. Check the yarns you are considering by twisting one strand of each together to see if they blend and look nice together.

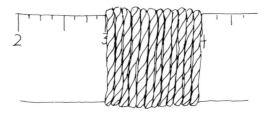

Number of yarns in 1" divided by half, or number of yarns in 5 cm (no dividing necessary).

Suggested yarns for a 10-dent heddle:
- any two-ply wool with 1200-1500 yards per pound (2400-3000 m/kg)
- 7/2 Swedish wool by Borgs or Berga (1566 yards/pound or 3150 m/kg)
- two-ply fine wool from Wilde Yarns (1280-1440 yards/pound or 2570-2900 m/kg) or Condon Yarns (1200 yards/pound or 2400 m/kg)
- Brown Sheep Top of the Lamb, wool size #2 (1200 yards/pound or 2400 m/kg)

Suggested yarns for an 8-dent heddle:
- any two- or three-ply wool at approximately 800 yards per pound (1600 m/kg)
- N2N wool from Ironstone Warehouse (760 yards/pound or 1530 m/kg)
- two-ply medium wool from Condon Yarns (800 yards/pound or 1600 m/kg)
- Brown Sheep Top of the Lamb, wool size #1 (784 yards/pound or 1580 m/kg)
- Lily Sugar 'n Cream cotton (800 yards/pound or 1600 m/kg)

If you can't find these specific yarns, you can substitute any smooth, strong, wool or cotton yarns of equivalent size.

Winding the yarn into balls. Some yarns are sold in skeins which must be wound into balls before you use them. Open up the skein, place it over your hands, and give it several sharp snaps to straighten and separate the strands so they will unwind easily. The skein should be held under light tension so it can unwind without tangling. Place the skein on an umbrella swift, around somebody's hands or knees, or on the back of a chair. Find the ends of the yarn and begin with the end which unwinds on the outside of the skein. Wind the yarn into a ball, using the winding method shown here or a ball winder.

To use an umbrella swift, fasten it to a table as shown. Open the skein and place it loosely around the cage. Move the spool-like piece just below the cage so it pushes the skein out to its full spread. Tighten the screw to hold the cage and yarn in this position. Find both ends of the yarn and choose the one which unwinds on the outside of the skein to begin your ball.

Fasten the ball winder to a table and feed one end of your yarn through the metal guide and slip it into the notches at the top of the plastic tube. Turn the handle in either direction, but once you've picked a direction keep using it until you finish the skein. The yarn will wind around the plastic tube. When you've finished winding, slide the ball off the top of the tube.

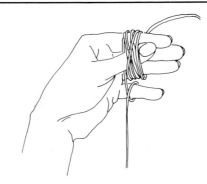

To wind a center-pull ball by hand, wrap the short end of the yarn around your little finger; this will be the end that will pull from the center of the ball   don't lose it! Begin to wind the yarn around your fingers. After you have wound a little, remove the ball from your fingers and rotate it a quarter turn. Wind some more, rotate, and keep repeating. Wind loosely or your ball won't pull from the center.

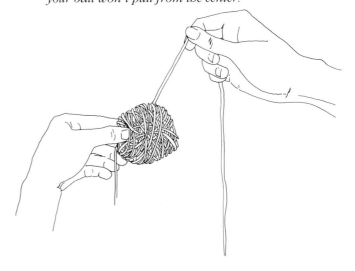

Pillow or Runner
Designed by Jean Scorgie

FABRIC DESCRIPTION: Plain weave with weft float pattern.

FINISHED SIZE: Pillow—13″ (32.5 cm) square with 5″ (12.5 cm) fringe on one end. **Runner**—13″ (32.5 cm) wide by 26″ (65 cm) long with 5″ (12.5 cm) fringe on each end.

WARP: 85% wool/15% mohair at 784 yd/lb (1570 m/kg). This is Top of the Lamb Mohair Blend from Brown Sheep Company, available in 196 yd (178 m)/4 oz skeins: 218 yd (198 m) Boysenberry #M55 (some used for weft).

WEFT: Singles wool at 784 yd/lb (1570 m/kg). This is Top of the Lamb, Size #1, from Brown Sheep Company, available in 196 yd (178 m)/4 oz skeins: 18 yd (16 m) Framboise #311, 25 yd (23 m) Seaglass #370.

Wool bouclé at 750 yd/lb (1500 m/kg). This is Tumbleweed from Wilde Yarns, available in 94 yd (85 m)/2 oz skeins: 21 yd (19 m) Bluegrass, used double.

E.P.I.: 8 (32/10 cm).

HEDDLE: 8-dent (32/10).

WIDTH IN HEDDLE: 14″ (34.5 cm).

TOTAL WARP ENDS: 112.

WEFT ROWS PER INCH: 8 (32/10).

TAKE-UP & SHRINKAGE: 7% in width and length.

WARP LENGTH: 54″ (135 cm), which includes take-up, shrinkage, and 18″ (45 cm) loom waste.

WEAVING: Weave 3 rows scrap yarn and beat them to within 1″ (2.5 cm) of the tie-on knots. Weave 2 more rows scrap yarn, leaving the warp evenly spaced. With Boysenberry, weave 8 or 9 rows ending on the up shed. Change sheds and with a pick-up stick in back of the heddles, pick up every other warp on the slot shed. Place the pick-up stick on edge and weave 3 rows of Seaglass in the pick-up shed, wrapping it around the edge warp on each row. Push the pick-up stick flat to the back of the loom.

With Boysenberry, weave 3 rows plain weave, breaking it after the last row and weaving the end in. Bring the pick-up stick forward on edge and weave 3 rows of Seaglass in the pick-up shed, breaking after the last row and weaving the end in. With Framboise, weave 9 rows plain weave and a triple row on the pick-up shed, ending the color. Using a double strand of Bluegrass, weave 9 rows in plain weave, weave a triple row on the pick-up shed with Framboise, weave 3 rows in plain weave with Bluegrass and end the color. Weave a triple row on the pick-up shed with Framboise and end the color.

With Boysenberry, weave 9 rows plain weave and a triple row on the pick-up shed, ending the color. With Seaglass, weave 13 rows plain weave, a triple row on the pick-up shed, 3 rows plain weave, a triple row on the pick-up shed, and end the color.

With Boysenberry, weave 5 rows plain weave. With Framboise, weave a triple row on the pick-up shed, ending the color. Continue with Boysenberry, weaving plain weave until the piece measures 14″ (34.5 cm) under tension (13″ [32.5 cm] relaxed). This is the middle of the runner and one-half of the pillow.

Make a template of the stripe placement under tension and reverse the order of colors for the second half. After the last row, weave 3 rows in scrap yarn. Cut the warp 6″ (15 cm) from the last row, untie the knots at the beginning, and remove from the loom.

ASSEMBLY: With a blunt needle, repair any skips and work in ends you overlooked during the weaving. Steam press lightly. For a runner, at each end remove four warps at a time from the rows of scrap yarn and tie them in an overhand knot. Trim both fringes 5″ (12.5 cm) long. For a pillow, fold the fabric in half, matching the stripes at the sides. Knot the warps together to close the lower edge of the pillow, removing two warps on each end from the scrap yarn and tying them together in an overhand knot. Thread a blunt needle with Boysenberry, whipstitch the selvedges together on one side of the pillow, insert a stuffed pillow form, and whipstitch the selvedges together on the other side. □

USING A TEMPLATE

A template helps you repeat an identical pattern accurately several times within a single piece. It also helps you weave several pieces of the same size (like place mats), or match the pattern on two pieces that will be joined.

Make a template from a 2-inch (5 cm) strip of paper or nonwoven interfacing material. Pin it along one edge of the weaving-in-progress with two pins. As you weave the first panel or design sequence, mark on the template any color or pattern changes. As the weaving progresses, move the bottom pin up to secure the template near the fell. When the template has been marked, use it to guide the placement of wefts in subsequent pieces.

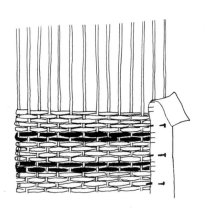

This introductory project will help you become familiar with the basics of weaving on a rigid heddle loom, including warping, weaving in balanced plain weave and with stripes, and adding a decorative float pattern. The finished project can be used as a runner or made into a cozy pillow.

15

Warping

After you've chosen the yarn, you need to measure lengths of yarn for warp and thread your loom with them. This is called *warping* or *dressing the loom*. Attention to details will get you off to a good start in weaving. Follow these procedures carefully on your first projects until you are familiar with all the steps. Warping variations are presented later, and a "Warping Procedure Quick Check" is in the appendix.

Measuring the warp

The first step in warping is to measure the individual threads, called *warp ends* or *ends*, that you will put on the loom to serve as the foundation for your weaving. Remember *tension?* A lot of tension problems can be created or prevented by the way you measure the warp ends and put them on the loom. The method described here will help you sidestep potential problems.

Make a *guide string* to help you measure the warp. Use string in a color which contrasts with your warp. Tie a loop in one end of the guide string and measure off the warp length, for this project 50 inches (125 cm), and mark it. Cut the guide string 12 inches or so (about 30 cm) longer so you'll have enough to tie around the warping peg or clamp. Using the string as a guide, set up your C-clamps or warping pegs at the appropriate distance or find the pathway around the pegs on your warping board that will give you the correct length.

By winding the yarn in a figure-eight at one end of the warp you will keep the threads in order; the "waist" of the figure-eight, where the threads cross each other, is called the *weaver's cross* or *warp cross*. As you measure the warp, you'll make this figure-eight at the place where you have two C-clamps set close together, or on the warping block with two pegs in it, or at the top or bottom of the warping board.

Tie the warp yarn onto the end peg *farthest* from where you will make the warp cross. Follow the path of the guide string to the pair of end pegs where you will make the cross.

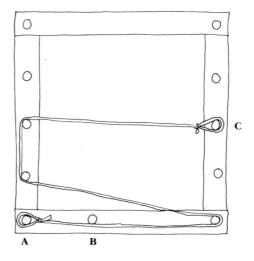

Establish the pathway around the pegs which will give you the appropriate length of warp. If you work with your warping board braced against a wall, you will find it easier to have pegs A and B at the top of the board. Small warping boards can be placed flat on a table.

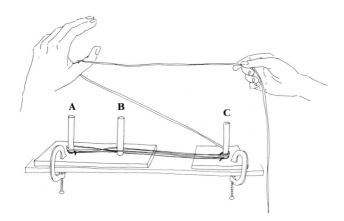

The distance between pegs A and C determines the length of your warp. Pegs will be clamped to a table or counter at the appropriate distance. The warp cross is made between pegs A and B.

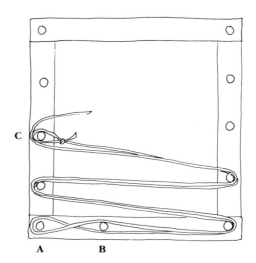

Make the warp cross by placing the warp *over* peg A and *under* peg B in one direction and by reversing on the return (over B and under A). Be sure to make the warp cross the *same way* each time and carefully place each turn next to the previous one on the pegs. The warp ends should lie flatly next to one another. If you look straight down at the top of the cross, you should see the warp ends alternating one by one.

Warping the loom and weaving will go more smoothly if you keep an even tension on the yarn while you wind it. This will be easy when you develop rhythm and speed through efficient hand motions. Place the ball of yarn on the floor or in a small box to your right. (Reverse all directions if you are left-handed, or if the reverse direction feels more comfortable.) The yarn will travel straight up from the ball through your right hand. Use this hand to maintain an even tension on the yarn at all times while the left hand guides the yarn back and forth around the pegs. If you need to take a break, simply wrap the yarn around a peg several times to maintain the tension.

A knot in the middle of the warp will cause problems when the heddle tries to pass over it—the knot will either get stuck in the heddle or it will break and have to be mended. If you come to a knot in the warp yarn, go back to the nearest end peg, cut out the section of yarn, and move the knot to this location. Your "intentional" knot will be behind the end peg.

Continue in this manner, stopping every few minutes to count the warps and tie them into bundles to help you keep track of how many yarns have been measured. Take a short length of contrasting string and lay it under the threads at the warp cross. Count 10 warp ends at the point where they cross. Bring the tails of the *counting string* up and tie a half-knot. Continue to wind the warp and to count groups of 10, using the same tails to tie each unit.

I suggest that you measure only one-half the total number of ends at a time. It's much easier to keep all threads the same length and under the same tension if you put the warp on the loom in narrow sections.

If you are using an 8-dent heddle, you will need 112 warp ends, or two groups of 56 ends. If you are using a 10-dent heddle, you will need 140 ends, or two groups of 70.

Before you remove the warp from the warping board it must be tied securely in several places. Do not include the guide string in the ties. At each end peg and on each side of the cross, use short lengths of string in a contrasting color to tie a loose bow knot around the warp. In addition, tie a *choke-tie* every yard along the length of the warp by wrapping the string two or three times around the warp yarns, cinching it up very tightly and securing it with a bow knot. I recommend bow knots because they are easy to untie. The tight choke-ties prevent the warp ends from slipping out of alignment while the loom is threaded, and they eliminate tangles while you wind the warp onto the beam.

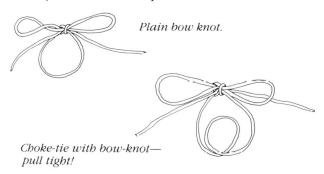

Plain bow knot.

Choke-tie with bow-knot— pull tight!

Use the illustration to carefully check the placement of your ties. When the warp is securely tied, remove your counting string and take the warp off the pegs, leaving the guide string in place for the second half of the warp.

Wind and tie the second half of the warp exactly as you did the first half.

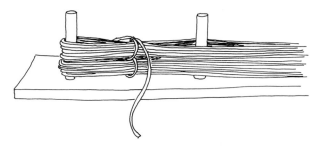

A counting string will help you keep track of how many warp ends have been measured.

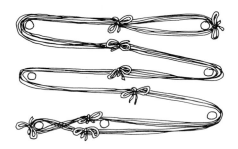

Choke ties will keep your warp in order as you transfer it to the loom.

Putting the warp on the loom

After you have measured the entire warp, you can begin to put it onto the loom. The technique described here is commonly referred to as the "back-to-front" method.

Here's an overview. You will first thread each warp loop through a slot in the heddle, and attach it to the warp beam. Then you will wind the warp onto the warp beam. The heddle will keep the warp threads evenly spaced so they will wind on smoothly. After winding on, you will remove one yarn from each slot and thread it through a hole. Finally, you will tie the yarns in groups to the cloth beam.

Pay particular attention to the detailed directions for hand motions, which will help you go faster.

Set the loom on a table or stand and place the heddle upright in the heddle holders provided with the loom. If your loom does not have heddle holders, attach a small C-clamp to the bottom of the heddle so it will stand upright. If your loom has plastic teeth on its beams, turn the teeth on the cloth beam so they face down; then the warp won't snag on them while you are working. The teeth on the warp beam should be slanted slightly away from you.

You can move the heddle closer if it will be easier to see. If heddle holders are a permanent part of your loom but are too far away for you to reach comfortably, attach a C-clamp to the heddle and bring it closer to you.

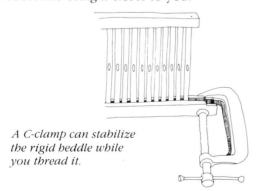

A C-clamp can stabilize the rigid heddle while you thread it.

Place the warp cross on your left hand. All four fingers go through the end loops and the thumb goes between the long tails. The cross should fit snugly around your fingers. If the loop is too big, pull the warps on each side of the cross to snug it up. Don't let your thumb slip out while you are working! When the cross is securely on your hand and you foresee no interruptions, remove the bow knot at the end. Slide the two ties on each side of the cross down to the first choke-tie. Then if your thumb does slip out you can still retrieve the cross. Do not untie any of the choke-ties yet. If you are interrupted, carefully remove the warp cross from your hand and drape it around something that will keep it in order.

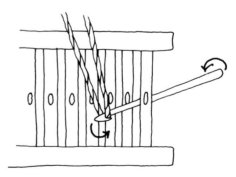

Hold the cross on your hand and pull off the top loop of warp.

To thread the loops through the slots of the heddle, start at the right side and work to the left. The width of the warp for this project is 14 inches (35 cm), so start in the slot to the right of the center mark which is labeled "7" (half of the width).[2] With the crochet hook, pick up the top warp at the cross and lift the loop from your hand. Hold the loop with your left hand and insert the crochet hook from the back of the heddle through this slot. Slip the loop under the hook and keep some tension on it as you swivel the crochet hook down through the slot. Carry the loop to the warp beam and drop it over the tooth with the corresponding mark. Pick up the next warp loop at the cross and pull it through the next slot. Don't bother about the holes yet.

Thread each loop through a slot in the heddle, moving from right to left.

---

[2]With a metric heddle, you will find the slot equivalent to 17.5 cm (your marks will be at 16 cm and 18 cm) and begin your warp there.

DOWEL RODS

If your loom has a dowel rod on each beam, instead of teeth, you will use a different method to attach your yarn to the warp and cloth beams. If the dowel rod is simply looped through the extension cords, remove it. If it is permanently attached, obtain one more dowel rod of the same length.

Use masking tape to fasten the loose dowel rod to the side of the loom so it sticks up at an angle. As each end loop is threaded through a slot, drop it over the dowel rod. Once all the warp loops have been threaded through the slots, unfasten the dowel rod, keeping the loops on it. Decide where the extension cord will rest in relation to the width of the warp.

If you are working with a single dowel rod, carefully slide onto your hand the group of loops between the first point where the extension cord will be and the edge. Slip the extension cord over the dowel rod and replace the group of end loops between there and the next point where the extension cord will rest. Continue until all the warp loops are evenly spread to the width of the warp and the extension cord holds the dowel rod parallel to the warp beam.

If you are working with an extra dowel rod, tie it snugly to the permanent dowel rod at both ends, using a strong cord. Spread the warp loops evenly to the desired width. You may want to put an additional tie or two evenly spaced across the center of the rods.

If you find it difficult to prop up the dowel rod, let the warp loops hang loose at the back of the heddle as you thread them. After all the loops have been threaded, pick up each one in order and slip it over the dowel rod, placing the extension cord as you go.

Proceed with winding on.

When it is time to tie the other end of the warp to the front beam, pick up about a 1-inch group of warps on one edge and smooth it out. Divide it in half, take both sections over the dowel rod, bring half up on each side of the group, and tie the sections together with a half-knot. Secure a 1-inch group on the other edge in the same way. Tie the rest of the groups, alternating from side to side and working toward the center.

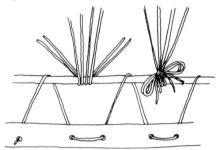

Weave the first rows with scrap yarn, adjust the tension on the groups, and then tie the other half of each knot.

When all the loops have been threaded through slots and attached to the warp beam, you're ready to wind the warp onto the back beam. Untie the bow knots near the cross, leaving only the choke-ties. Grasp each warp section at its first choke-tie and give it a couple of sharp shakes. Be careful not to dislodge the loops from the teeth on the warp beam! Hang on to the loom so you don't jerk it off the table. The warp will straighten out. If necessary, work any loose yarns down to the choke-tie by stroking the warp between your fingers and thumb. Repeat this motion several times until all the warp ends are even. It is not necessary to comb the warp with your fingers. In fact, combing can make the warp ends more uneven. Gently lay the warp sections down over the cloth beam.

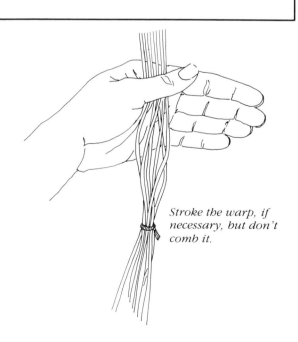

Stroke the warp, if necessary, but don't comb it.

Line up the edge of the brown paper with the warp beam and start winding. Be sure the edge threads don't slide off the paper. Make two turns, then stop and secure the warp beam with the ratchet or knob. Grasp each warp chain just above the choke-tie and pull it down over the front beam until the warp around the back beam is tight. Each warp section must be tightened equally. Repeat the winding and tightening process until the first choke-ties come close to the front beam.

Pull each warp chain with even tension to tighten it.

Stop and make sure the back beam has been secured so it won't unwind. On each warp chain, remove the first choke-tie, then grasp the warp just above the next choke-tie and shake it to smooth the warp. Continue winding. Stop every two turns of the warp beam to straighten and tighten the warp. Insert new sheets of paper as needed. You're finished winding on when 6 inches (15 cm) of warp remain in front of the cloth beam. Cut the end loops and remove the last choke-ties.

Now you can finish threading the heddle. Starting on the right side, remove one of the warp ends from the first slot and thread it through the hole next to it with the crochet hook. As you pull the warp out of the slot, loop it over your finger. Insert the crochet hook into

the heddle hole from the front and drop the warp loop over the hook, keeping tension on the loop as you pull the crochet hook through the hole. Move the pair of warps out of the way to the right. Repeat this process across the warp. Generally, using the hole to the left of the slot is easier, but it doesn't matter which direction you go as long as you are consistent.

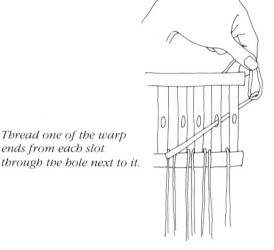

Thread one of the warp ends from each slot through the hole next to it.

Tie the warp ends onto the cloth beam. The warp ends must travel absolutely straight from the warp beam, to the cloth beam, or you will have problems when you start to weave. The marks you made on the beams will simplify this.

If it is not already there, move the heddle back against the shed blocks or place it in the holders. Lay the warp ends in pairs evenly spaced between the teeth on the cloth beam. If the edge warps start at number 7 in the heddle, lay them in the slot marked 7 on the cloth beam. The way the warp ends lie between the teeth will depend on the size of your heddle and the number of teeth per inch on the beam. Your marks will make figuring this out a matter of visual alignment, not math. If you are using an 8-dent heddle and have five teeth per inch (2.5 cm), you will put two warp ends each in four out of five spaces in every inch-wide section of the beams.

PLACE THE HEDDLE IN THE UP SHED POSITION on top of the shed blocks. This is important! This makes the warps in the heddle holes slightly longer than the warps in the slots. If you forget to place the heddle in the up shed position when you tie on, the warps in the holes will be too tight when you weave. (If the heddle won't stand upright by itself, tie the two outside groups first, then place the heddle in the up shed.)

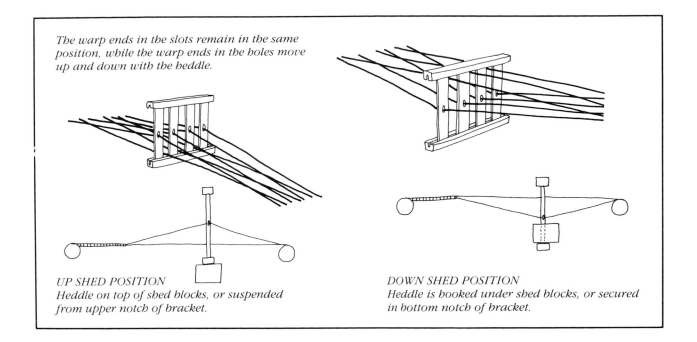

The warp ends in the slots remain in the same position, while the warp ends in the holes move up and down with the heddle.

UP SHED POSITION
Heddle on top of shed blocks, or suspended from upper notch of bracket.

DOWN SHED POSITION
Heddle is hooked under shed blocks, or secured in bottom notch of bracket.

Take about 8 of the warps, those lying in four slots, smooth them out, and tie a half-knot around the teeth. Tie the two outside groups first, then alternate from side to side, working toward the center. When you finish, the tension will probably need adjusting. Start in the center this time and alternate from side to side, working out to the selvedges, which will probably be a little looser than the rest. Adjust each tie by cinching its tails up a little before you secure the ends with a bow knot. It's important when you tie these knots to exert the same amount of tension on each tie. Do this step quickly at one sitting, without interruption. Keep your hands below the level of the cloth beam so the warps don't pop out of the slots.

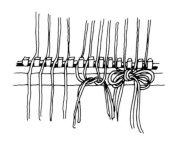

To check the tension, close your eyes and gently pat the warp to feel if there are any tight or loose groups. Adjust those groups. Any unevenness in the tension that is not corrected at this point will show up in the first few rows of weaving and can be fixed then. You're ready to weave!

THE KEYS TO SUCCESSFUL WARPING ARE:

- to keep an even tension while winding the warp on the warping board,
- to keep an even tension on each warp section while winding the warp onto the back beam, and
- to keep an even tension while tying onto the front beam.

Beginning to Weave

Place the loom so it is secure and comfortable for you. Practice opening the sheds and handling the heddle. To make a shed in the up position, raise the heddle and set it on top of the shed blocks. To make a shed in the down position, push the heddle down and hook its ends under the block. On a loom with brackets, the top notch makes a shed in the up position, the center notch makes no shed, and the bottom notch makes a shed in the down position. The warp should be tight enough to hold the heddle in place. The tension on the warp doesn't need to be extremely tight, just enough to hold the heddle in place while still allowing the sheds to open easily.

Bring the heddle forward to beat a weft into place. Always use both hands and keep the heddle parallel to the cloth beam. Before you return the heddle to the shed block, start changing the shed by lifting the heddle up as you move it back and place it on top of the shed blocks or in the upper bracket notch. Bring the heddle forward to beat. Then change the shed again by pushing down on the heddle as you move it back to hook it under the shed blocks or place it in the lower bracket position.

Some yarns tend to stick to each other. Changing the shed as the heddle is moved back helps separate the yarns to make a clear shed. If some of the yarns still stick together, flick your finger across the upper layer and they will spring apart.

Wind one of your shuttles with about 6 feet (200 cm) of scrap yarn for the first rows of weaving. When the piece comes off the loom, these rows will be removed. To wind a shuttle, fasten the yarn around the notches at one end of the shuttle in a figure-eight. Then wind the yarn lengthwise around the shuttle, winding it over your fingers to put a little ease in the yarn. When you remove your fingers, the yarn should be relaxed.

When you are ready to fill a shuttle with yarn for your project, don't fill it too full or it will be hard to push the shuttle through the shed when you weave. If you are using wool, break the yarn instead of cutting it, when the shuttle is full. The tapered ends will make smooth joins.

Weaving the first rows

Before you weave with the weft yarn for your project, you need to weave a few rows with scrap yarn to space the warps evenly. Weave as many rows as seem necessary, usually from three to eight, and beat them down in groups, as follows.

Place the heddle in the up position. Pass the shuttle with the scrap yarn through the shed in front of the heddle. The widest part of the shed is next to the heddle. If you get in the habit of running the shuttle through at this point, there is less chance that the shuttle will skip a warp end and make a mistake in your fabric. Pull the yarn through, leaving 1 inch (2.5 cm) sticking out at the edge where you started. For these first rows, don't beat until you have woven three rows. Beating three rows at once creates friction between the warp and weft which helps the warp ends spread more evenly than if you beat after each row. Change to the down shed, put the shuttle through again, return to the up shed, and weave through once more. Beat down all three rows at the same time by picking up the heddle with both hands and bringing it straight forward to press the rows close to the knots or teeth.

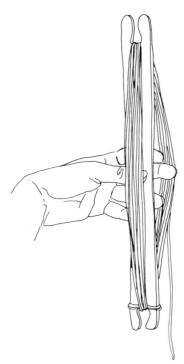

Winding a stick shuttle.

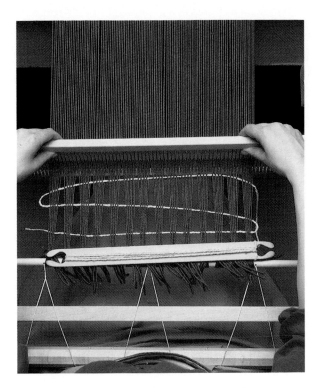

Weave three rows with scrap yarn and beat them down all at once. Place your shuttle on the weaving at the front of the loom, and be sure to bring the heddle squarely forward when you beat.

Repeat the whole heading sequence (three wefts and beating) once. If the warp yarns still aren't evenly spaced, you may have to do another sequence. If three rows are extremely hard to beat down, use two in each repeat.

The edge of the woven cloth where you have placed the most recent weft thread is called the *fell*. If the fell is straight, the tension is even—congratulations! A hump at the fell indicates a section of warp that is too loose; a hollow indicates a section that is too tight. Untie the bow knot for any group that needs adjusting. If the group is too loose, pull on the tails of the knot until the fell line straightens out and retie the knot. If a group is too tight, wiggle the knot a little to loosen it until the fell levels out. It is easy to correct uneven tension in these first few rows; however, tension problems which may develop later can also be adjusted. (See "Troubleshooting" in the appendix.)

Watch the fell as you weave. If the outside warp ends loosen up in the weaving process—which may mean that you're snagging them with the shuttle as you put it into the shed—the fell will tell you. When you fix tension problems quickly your weaving will go smoothly.

The fell will also tell you if you are bringing the heddle forward squarely when you beat. After they have been beaten into place, the weft threads should lie at a 90-degree angle to the warp.

You are ready to start weaving with your project weft when the warp yarns are neatly spaced and the fell is straight, indicating that each warp yarn is under the same amount of tension as all the others.

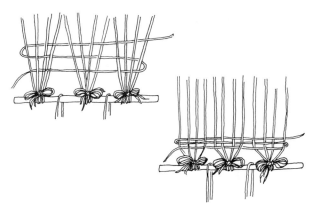

When you weave the first rows, insert three wefts of scrap yarn before you beat. This evens out the spacing of the warp yarns.

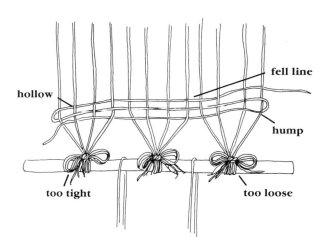

Unevenness at the fell line tells you that you need to tighten or loosen groups of warp ends.

Handling shuttles

Open the shed and pass the weft yarn shuttle through the shed, running it just in front of the heddle, and leaving a 1-inch (2.5 cm) tail hanging as before. This time you will beat each row into place individually and you will tuck the tail in on the second shed.

When you take the shuttle from the shed, leave the yarn in the shed at an angle. Put the shuttle down in front of you. Pick up the heddle with both hands and bring it toward you to press the weft in place. Move the heddle to the opposite shed position. Tuck the tail into the new shed with your fingers. Pass the shuttle through this shed in the other direction, and press the second weft into place.

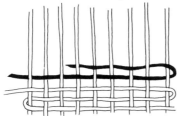

As you weave the second row of weft yarn, tuck in the tail from the first row.

It is very important to have the weft in the shed at an angle. A diagonal weft is longer than one laid in directly across the fell, and this extra length lets the weft yarn undulate over and under the warp threads. If you weave without angling your weft, your fabric will become narrower and narrower. A little *draw-in,* or narrowing, is normal, and the amount will vary according to the yarn you are using. If your weaving draws in more than ½ inch (1.25 cm) on each side, however, the strain on the outside warp threads will cause them to fray and break.

Each time the shuttle has passed through the shed, flick the end to release more weft for the next row. Avoid end-for-ending the shuttle since this wastes motion. Don't unwind too much yarn or you will spend time drawing extra weft through each shed.

Even edges

The *selvedges* are the edges of the fabric. They are also the place where the weft thread comes out of one shed, turns, and enters the next shed. Neat, even selvedges are a hallmark of good craftsmanship; they require practice on any loom, but there are special techniques that will help you make even selvedges on a rigid heddle loom.

The first step toward straight selvedges is to find the angle at which to lay your weft in the sheds. You will need to try various angles in the first inch or so of weaving and to watch your edges. An angle which is too steep makes loops in the weft; an angle which is too shallow pulls

After you place the second row of weft but before you beat it into place, tuck the tail of yarn into the shed.

in the edges of your fabric. Once you know the best angle, use it consistently. On your next piece, the angle may be different since it depends on the yarns you are using.

The way the weft enters each shed also affects the selvedges. Because the shed on a rigid heddle loom is shallow, the yarn makes a rounded turn instead of tightly bending around the outside warp. This is especially true with thicker wefts. Unless you know how to get the weft to lie neatly, you will get a loop of weft at the edge that doesn't look good, instead of a snug, even selvedge.

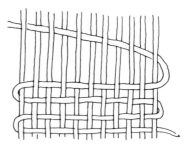

The way the weft yarn turns around the edge warp will affect the evenness of the edges of your weaving.

After passing the shuttle through the shed, pull the weft down to the fell line on the edge where the shuttle entered. Draw the excess through the shed so the weft is snug around the edge and makes a sharp angle. It shouldn't be so tight that it pulls the warp in, nor so loose that it leaves a loop. Make sure the rest of the weft lies loosely in the shed at an angle. When you beat the weft in, the edge loop will stay right where you want it, and you'll have beautiful, straight edges.

Don't fuss too much over this technique—just keep working on it until the motion becomes quick and fluid.

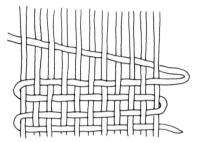

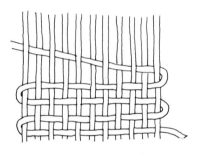

To get a neat edge, pull the weft down to the fell line in a sharp angle and then draw it through the shed until it fits neatly, but not tightly, around the edge warp.

As yarns interlace, they don't go in straight lines. They move around each other. For this reason, a weaving will draw in *(weft direction) and* take up *(warp direction) and be slightly smaller than the measurements of the warp in the heddle and on the warping board. Draw-in can be kept to a minimum if you angle the weft in the shed.*

An even beat

One goal of this first project is to give you practice in making a balanced weave fabric, where there are the same number of weft rows per inch as there are warp threads. To find out if you are beating hard enough to make a balanced weave fabric, lay a ruler on your fabric and count the number of weft rows in one inch. There should be 10 rows in an inch if you are using a 10-dent heddle, or 8 if you are using an 8-dent heddle (the same number of warps in one inch). If your fabric has more, you are beating too hard—lighten up and don't press so hard. If you don't have enough weft rows in each inch, press a little harder. You can control the force of each beat. With a little practice, you will develop a rhythm and be able to beat consistently.

Periodically count the number of weft rows per inch, especially if you have taken a break. Your motions may be different when you return to the loom and you may be beating harder or lighter than before. You want the beat to be even throughout the piece.

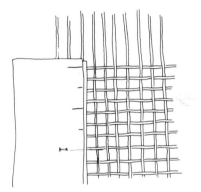

Starting a new shuttle

Eventually you will run out of yarn on the shuttle. Weave up to the last bit and lay it in the shed as far as it will go, even though it may end in the middle. Beat it down and open the *same* shed again. Fill the shuttle with more of the same color. Pass the new shuttle through until the two ends overlap about an inch (2.5 cm).

If you are weaving with wool and broke the end of your yarn instead of cutting it, you will be rewarded at this point. The tapered fibers will make an invisible join.

Some colors and a pattern

One of the easiest ways to add interest to weaving is to use stripes of different colors in the weft.

JOINING COTTON AND OTHER FIRM YARNS

If you are using a firm yarn like cotton you will have to cut the yarn and use a different method to conceal the join. Before you lay the last bit of yarn in the shed, untwist the end of it to separate the plies. Weave. Pull one strand of the separated end up between two warp ends where you want the join to occur. Untwist the end of the new weft yarn and pull the yarn into the shed so its end overlaps the end of the old weft. Pull one of its strands out

of the shed and let it dangle. After you have woven a few rows, trim off the loose ends.

This technique lets you overlap the ends and maintain the same yarn diameter in the shed. The joins may or may not be noticeable; after you have made one or two, look to see if they're unobtrusive. If not, make the joins near the selvedge where they will be less conspicuous.

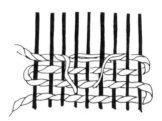

Stripes. To make a stripe, just change your weft color. There are several ways to hide the tails when you change colors, but in balanced weaves you can overlap the old and new ends at a selvedge just like you did when you ran out of yarn. Breaking the old yarn can be tricky, because you want to end up with a tail which extends only an inch (2.5 cm) past the selvedge. If the yarn's tail is more than an inch long, it will show too much in your finished weaving. Try pulling on the yarn with your fingers several inches apart. If the yarn won't break, untwist it a little and break each strand separately. If you are using a synthetic or strong cotton yarn, you will need to cut it. Snip the end at an angle or cut the individual plies at different lengths to make a tapered end.

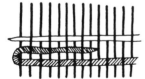

Open a new shed and tuck the tail of the old color into it. Overlap the next color, placing its end right at the selvedge. If the yarns are soft, the change in color will not be noticeable.

The project includes stripes of different widths so you can practice beginnings and endings. If you forget to break off a color and tuck the tail in, you can pull the end into the shed where it belongs later with a crochet hook or a blunt tapestry needle.

Narrow stripes. Narrow stripes of only two or three rows don't need to have the old color broken each time you want to change. The unused color can be carried along the edge warp and enclosed by the new weft so it doesn't show.

Use a stick inserted behind the heddle to make a decorative float pattern (see p. 27). The first set of floats has been woven and another is being started.

Weave a row with color A. Change sheds and weave color B in the same direction. Change sheds, tuck in the tail, and weave with color B as you hold color A alongside the edge warp thread so it's included in the weft loop. When not in use, place one of the shuttles on the weaving and the other on the table or in your lap. Setting each shuttle in its own place helps prevent the wefts from tangling. Weave two rows with color A while you hold color B along the edge warp. You will be able to do this quickly, but you have to remember to do it or you will get loops that float along the edge. Don't use this method of carrying a color for more than half an inch (1.25 cm); if you won't be using the carried color soon it is best to break the yarn off and tuck in its end.

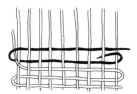

Alternating colors. When you want to alternate two colors row by row, another trick will come in handy. The two wefts must interlock when they start from the same selvedge or the edge warp will not be woven. If the last weft comes out *over* the top of the edge warp, the next weft color has to go *over* that weft before it enters the shed. If the last weft comes out *under* the edge warp, the next shuttle will have to go *under* that weft before it enters the shed. Remember: *over/over* and *under/under*. Any time you alternate colors row by row you will have to interlock the wefts at the selvedge.

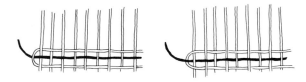

A float pattern. There's lots of fun to be had with a pick-up stick. You can give your fabric some surface texture by making a series of weft floats. The idea is simple, but the hundreds of possible variations could keep your shuttle flying for years.

As you remember, only the warps threaded in the heddle holes move up and down. The warps in the slots stay in the same position because they are not attached to anything. The positions of these passive warps can be changed with a pick-up stick. If you use the stick *behind* the

heddle, you can leave it there until you need it, and the heddle will still move up and down for plain weave.

After weaving a row in the up shed, place the heddle in the *down* shed position. This puts the slot threads in the upper layer. Insert a strip of cardboard or paper in the shed behind the heddle to block out your view of the lower layer so you can count the warps in the slot layer easily. Only the warps in the slot layer will be picked up with the pick-up stick. Insert the pick-up stick under one thread, then over one. (Although our project uses this float sequence, you may want to use one up, two down on some warps set at 10 ends per inch, to make longer floats.) *Always pick up the edge warps on each side*, even if the pattern doesn't require them to be up. Otherwise the edges will not weave. Now remove the cardboard.

A piece of paper inserted behind the heddle will help you see only the slot layer threads as you insert the pick-up stick.

Once you've inserted a pick-up stick, its name changes; it is now called a *pattern stick*. To use it to make weft floats, leave the heddle in *neutral* position (in front of the shed block or in the center notch of a bracket). Bring the pattern stick forward behind the heddle and turn it on edge. This will make a shed you haven't seen before, and if you put the weft through it you will get a pattern of weft threads floating over the warps. Weave this row, turn the stick flat, and beat the weft into place with the heddle.

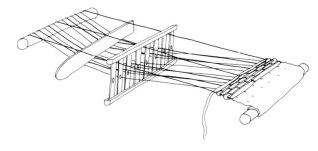

When you want to use the pattern shed, move the pick-up stick forward and turn it on edge.

Use the pattern-stick shed in place of the down shed, alternating it with the regular up shed. You can make the floats more prominent if you pass the shuttle back and forth several times in the same shed, catching the weft around the edge warp. Repeat this as many times as you want, or the directions specify, laying the weft at an angle and beating it down each time. When you have enough weft floats, move the pattern stick toward the warp beam where it will be out of the way. Weave a row in the *up* shed again and press it down tightly to puff up the floats.

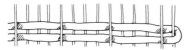

The float pattern occurs when weft threads skip over warps with which they would normally interweave.

The sequence is: up shed, pattern stick shed, up shed.

Although the first project uses all the pick-up wefts in sets of three, you can, for variety, make these heavy ridges with larger or smaller numbers of wefts. You can use them within colored stripes to add interest, in the same color as the stripe or a contrasting color. When you use a contrasting color of yarn for the floats, secure the end in the regular down shed.

Advancing the warp

After you have woven 4 or 5 inches (10 to 12 cm), you will need to wind the warp forward. Ideally, you should wind the warp forward when your weaving is halfway between the front beam and the shed blocks. As the fell gets closer to the heddle, the stress on the warp increases and there is not enough room to lay the weft in the shed at a good angle.

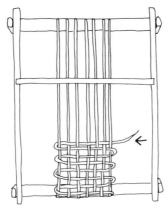

When your fell line is halfway between the cloth beam and the rigid heddle, advance the warp.

To wind the warp forward, place the loom flat on the table; a loom on a stand doesn't need to be moved, but set the heddle in the heddle holder. Loosen the back knobs or ratchet, unwind the warp beam a turn or two, and secure the warp beam again. *This is very important;* if you don't secure the warp beam, the whole warp may unwind. Loosen the front knobs or ratchet and wind the fabric forward. As the fabric starts to wind on top of the knots, lay in a strip of paper 4 inches (10 cm) wide to make a smooth surface for the fabric to rest on.

Finishing

Removing the fabric

When you're finished weaving, break the weft yarn off and tuck its tail into the last shed. Weave three or four rows with scrap yarn to keep the weft in place until you can secure the warp ends. Cut the warps at the back of the loom, leaving at least 4 inches (10 cm) of warp extending from the weaving. Unroll and untie the weaving from the front beam.

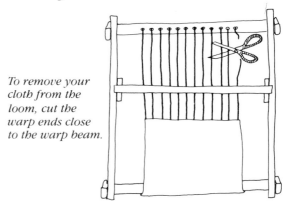

To remove your cloth from the loom, cut the warp ends close to the warp beam.

Correcting skips

Examine your woven piece carefully to see if there are any places where a yarn skips threads that it shouldn't. These skips can be repaired.

Thread a tapestry needle with some of the weft yarn. Break or cut the yarn so it has a tapered end. Find a weft row which skipped when it should have been woven. Start the needle ½ inch (1.25 cm) to the side of the skip and insert the needle along the pathway of that weft through the warp. When you come to the skip, move the needle the way the weft *should* have gone and continue for ½ inch (1.25 cm) on the other side of the float. Pull the yarn through until the tapered end is worked in. Snip off the other end and snip out the float. You've corrected the mistake!

If there are several floats along the same line, correct them all with the same mending yarn. Clip off and remove the weft which skipped. Warp floats can be fixed in the same way.

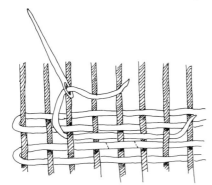

Correct a skip by weaving in a matching yarn along the path the weft should have taken.

Final touches

Secure the warp ends with *overhand knots*, which make a very easy finish. Lay the weaving on a table, with its fringe toward you. Place a heavy object, like a book, on the weaving to hold it in place while you work.

Beginning at either selvedge, use a crochet hook to gently pull each of the first four warp ends out of the scrap yarn. Holding the four ends together, make a loop, bring the tails through the loop, and push the loop up against the edge of the weaving, holding it there while you pull the tail tight. Work across the fabric, tying four ends at a time, then turn the fabric around and knot the other end. You can trim the fringe as long as you want, but no shorter than ¼ inch (5 mm). Trim the fringe by setting the fabric on a table, smoothing the fringe, and cutting it evenly with a sharp scissors.

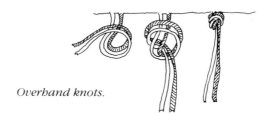

Overhand knots.

If the fabric is wool, gently hand wash it in warm water and liquid dishwashing soap. Treat it as you would a special sweater; don't run water directly onto it, don't subject it to very hot water or extreme temperature changes, and don't scrub it. Rinse the fabric well in warm water. To speed the drying process, roll the weaving in a terrycloth towel and squeeze it or put the weaving in the washing machine on a *spin-only* cycle. Smooth the fabric out on a flat surface to dry. Press it while it's slightly damp, using a damp pressing cloth and a steam iron.

If the fabric is cotton, you can machine wash and dry it. Remove the fabric from the dryer while it is still damp and smooth it out on a flat surface to dry. Iron it while it is damp; you won't need to use a pressing cloth.

The fabric is ready to be used as a table runner. If you'd like to make it into a pillow, fold the fabric in half with the "best" side inside, matching the stripes at the edges. Remove two warps on each end from the scrap yarn and tie them together in an overhand knot; this will close one edge of the pillow. Stitch together one other side of the pillow. Turn the pillow right side out, insert a stuffed pillow form, and whip-stitch the selvedges together on the final edge.

Enjoy your first weaving with pride! Start planning your second project right away; this is just the beginning. There's a lot to explore on the rigid heddle loom.

Discovering Plain Weave

Here are some ideas to get your own thoughts moving, along with projects to help you use those ideas. You could spend years happily and successfully discovering ways to use one heddle and the basic plain weave structure. Plain weave may be simple, but it is far from plain.

Plain weave is the most basic weaving construction: the yarns cross at right angles, interweaving in a pattern of "over one, under one." With plain weave you can produce the tightest, firmest fabric possible, although you can also make a light and airy cloth. There are so many ways to vary plain weave through choice of yarn, spacing, and color that its possibilities are unlimited.

Sett

Sett is a weaver's word which refers to the spacing of the warp ends in the heddle or reed. Each warp yarn can be used at a variety of setts, but the resulting fabrics will be different. Your first project was in a balanced weave. For example, at a sett of 8 (8 warps per inch, or 32/10) you wove about 8 picks per inch (2.5 cm). If you had set the same warp yarn at 5 ends per inch (20/10) and beaten just as firmly, the weft threads would have packed down over the warp, possibly covering it completely. You would have had more weft picks per inch and the fabric you produced—where the weft could be seen but the warp could not—would have been called **weft-faced.** If you had set that warp at 12 ends per inch (48/10) and maintained your beat, you wouldn't have gotten as many weft picks per inch because the warp would have resisted. If the warp covered the weft entirely, your fabric would have been called **warp-faced.**

The relationship between the warp and the weft can be balanced, or it can vary anywhere between the two extremes of weft-faced and warp-faced. The samples illustrating this idea have all been woven with the same size yarn, in different colors, for warp and weft. The only difference between the samples is the spacing of the warp—the sett—which affects the spacing of the weft. As the relationship between warp and weft changes, so does the color emphasis. Both these types of change offer us many possibilities for designing with plain weave.

Balanced Weave

Balanced weaves are an important classification. They have equal strength and elasticity in both directions. These are important qualities for those textiles, like garment fabrics, that need to be flexible and to drape well.

A *quick and easy way to estimate the sett* of a yarn for balanced weave involves the ruler-wrapping technique we used to check our selection of yarns for the first project. Wind a length of yarn around a ruler to cover 1 inch (2.5 cm). Let each strand lie snugly against its neighbors. Count the number of wraps in the inch and divide by two for the approximate number of **ends per inch** (also known as **EPI**) at which this yarn should be set. You could just wind half an inch and count the wraps, but the full inch gives a more accurate estimate.

Even rather subtle variations in the spacing of the warp and weft affect the quality, or **hand,** of the finished cloth. You can choose to make your fabric stiffer or softer as you select your sett.

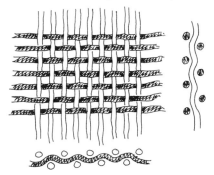

A balanced weave fabric.

If the calculated sett of a particular yarn is slightly higher than the spacing of your heddle (11 or 12 ends per inch instead of 10), that yarn will make a fairly loose weave if you use it at 10 ends per inch because the warp will be spaced a little farther apart than your estimate indicates. Depending on the character of the yarn you are using, this extra "air" will make your fabric either soft, drapable, and slightly sheer, or limp and sleazy. If the yarn is textured, rough, or hairy, this looser sett may be advantageous because the yarn itself will fluff up to fill in the extra space; the fibers tend to cling together and hold the yarns steady. If the yarn is very smooth

or hard—like most cottons or linens—the warps and wefts will shift around after the fabric is off the loom. You can check the effect by releasing the tension during weaving to see if any loosely placed rows slide around. Cottons and linens will shrink when they are washed; a certain amount of "air space" in the newly woven but unfinished fabric is appropriate, or the cloth will be too firm after it is washed. Too much "air space," however, will result in a flimsy cloth.

If the calculated sett is *much* higher than the spacing available on your heddle—say the yarn should be set at more than 12 EPI (48/10) and you have a 10-dent (40/10) heddle—that yarn is too fine to make a balanced weave with your heddle. Many cottons and silks will give you lots of wraps per inch. If you want to use such a yarn, try doubling it and using two strands as one. When you calculate your new sett, remember to count each *doubled* strand as one wrap. There are other ways to use fine yarn which we'll consider later.

A yarn that has a calculated sett slightly lower than the spacing of your heddle (9 EPI instead of 10, for example) will make a more closely woven fabric if set at 10 ends per inch. The warp will be set more tightly than might be ideal; if you beat the weft hard to maintain a balanced weave your fabric will be firm, crisp, stiff, or boardy, again depending on the yarn you are using. Slick yarns, like silk or rayon, may need to be set more tightly so they won't shift around.

If the calculated sett is significantly less than the spacing of your heddle (6 or 7 EPI instead of

How closely yarns are set affects the fabric structure and can affect the color emphasis. These samples were woven with a striped warp and a single-color weft of the same weight.

From narrowest to widest, they were produced by using:
  28 E.P.I. (a warp-faced fabric)
  16 E.P.I. (a warp-emphasis fabric)
  12 E.P.I. (a balanced weave)
  8 E.P.I. (a weft-emphasis fabric)
  6 E.P.I. (a weft-faced fabric)
The specific setts that result in each type of fabric vary with the yarns used. Each type of fabric is discussed in detail in this chapter.

10), the yarn is too heavy to make a balanced weave with that heddle. You can use it in a warp-faced or warp-emphasis fabric, which we will discuss soon, or you can use it as weft with a different warp—or, if your test suggests 7 EPI, you can try an 8-dent (32/10) heddle.

Textured yarns

Textured or novelty yarns make a quick change in the way a plain weave fabric looks. There are slubs, bumps, loops, knots, and snarls in some yarns; fibers can be spun into boucles or can be brushed; chenilles are slinky, and tweeds are rough. Textured yarns can be magical, but there are tricks to using them successfully. Some are beautiful in the skein but lose their character when woven. Others beat down more closely than their smooth counterparts and may produce a fabric which looks more like terry cloth than you intended. A few experiments will help you determine how best to show a textured yarn to its advantage.

Begin by choosing two yarns of similar size, one textured and one smooth. Warp your loom with the smooth yarn. First use the textured yarn alone as a weft; next weave alternate rows of the smooth and the textured yarns; then weave two rows of the smooth yarn to one of the textured; and then use three rows of the smooth to one of textured. You can also weave a sample with the textured yarn incorporated at random intervals. As you can see, smaller amounts of the different yarn can sometimes be more attractive.

Once you have found a pleasing combination of plain and textured wefts, you may decide that you would like the texture to run the length of the warp, instead of in the weft. You can do this if your textured yarn is strong enough. Pull a length of it between your hands and then give it a couple of tugs; to serve as warp it will have to withstand the loom's tension and to be moved forward through the heddles without breaking. If your yarn can handle this treatment, you can transfer the sequence of yarns from the weft to a warp. Count the **picks** or rows of weft (three smooth, one textured, for example) and measure and thread your warp to match. Then weave with a smooth yarn—or use a similar pattern of textured and smooth yarns in the weft as well, for a textured plaid effect.

Sometimes textured yarns are very fine. If you want to use one of these in a balanced weave with a heavier yarn, you can strand it together with another fine yarn of smooth texture. Aim for a combination where the two fine yarns together are the same size as the heavier yarn.

Grouped yarns

You can change the look of your fabric while using only one type of plain, smooth yarn if you group two or more strands together at intervals within the plain weave structure. This is also a way to use a yarn which seems too fine for your heddle. Yarns can be grouped in either warp or weft, or in both. The thicker areas will give texture to the surface of your weaving—as the

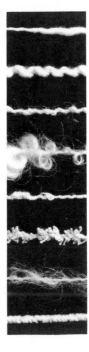

The swatch on the left, a study for the placemats described on pages 34-35, shows how a small amount of textured yarn can be very effective. The novelty yarns on the right, from bottom to top, are:
a chenille
a brushed yarn
a snarl
a knot
a loop
a bouclé
a bumpy yarn,
*   or spiral*
a slub.

float pattern did on the first project—and the variation will make shadows and highlights appear, making it look as though you used several closely related shades of yarn. When light comes from behind a fabric with grouped yarns, as it would in a lampshade or a curtain, the clusters show up as darker or denser areas. This effect is easier to obtain by grouping yarns.

To group yarns in the weft, weave back and forth in the same shed the appropriate number of times, as you did on the float pattern of your first project. Be sure to catch the weft around the outside warp on each pass so it won't pull out of the shed.

When you group yarns, you will have to play with the sett to find what will work best. Because warp ends in a group take up less space than they would if used singly, the overall number of ends per inch can be higher than normal. For instance, two warps grouped together will take up less space than if they work separately; there's no "air space" between them when they move together.

If you want to use a fine yarn in your heddle —for instance, one which should give a balanced weave at 14 EPI in your 10-dent heddle—you can double warp ends at regular intervals. In this example, you would double four threads in every inch. You can place the doubled ends at regular intervals or make a more complicated pattern of them.

When you want to place more than two or three warp ends in a group, you may need to skip spaces in your heddle to accommodate these larger bundles of yarn. If you want to make a group of four or more yarns, skip a hole and split the grouped yarns between the two adjacent slots. As another example, if you want six warps together you can thread three in one slot, skip a hole, and three in the next slot. These six threads will work as one "end" in three normal spaces; the three-plus-three slot yarns will weave together because there is no warp end in the hole between them. You can group yarns in either holes (if they'll fit) or slots.

Just as this technique will let you use finer yarns than your heddle normally accepts, a variation of it can help you use slightly heavier yarns. If you have a 10-dent heddle and want to use a yarn which should be set at 9 EPI for a balanced weave, you can skip one hole or slot in every inch. The two warp ends next to the skipped space will weave as one and will add some texture to your fabric, but you will be able to work with the yarn at 9 EPI. When you are experimenting with this, you can make a quick change if you find the spacing is too tight by clipping out a warp, pulling it out of the heddle toward the back, and letting it dangle from the back beam.

Spaced yarns

The opposite of grouping is leaving wide spaces. When you thread the heddle, periodically skip a number of spaces. You will find when you weave that the warps at the edges of the spaces will tend to creep into the spaces and fill them. A rough or textured weft yarn will help hold the warps in place. Some dramatic effects can occur as the spaces become wider; you will discover them when you try a number of different types of wefts. A rayon yarn will drape across the space. A heavy, soft weft yarn will puff out of the space and give the illusion of a warp stripe.

The weft can also be spaced, if you beat lightly where you want openness and harder in areas you want to look solid. You can also weave thin dowel rods into your fabric as weft spacers, pulling the dowels out before the fabric winds around the cloth beam.

The red fabric, used in the vest project on pages 82-83, is an example of grouped yarns. The yellow fabric demonstrates one use of spaced yarns.

These placemats are machine washable and dryable, so you can use them every day. The warp is a simple stripe pattern and the weft alternates smooth and textured cotton.

Placemats

Designed by Betty Davenport

FABRIC DESCRIPTION: Plain weave.

FINISHED SIZE: Six placemats, each 12¼" (30.6 cm) wide × 17½" (44 cm) long.

WARP: 8/2 cotton at 3575 yd/lb (7160 m/kg). This is Cotton Clouds Aurora Earth, available in 4470 yd (4067 m)/1¼ lb tubes: 200 yd (182 m) orange #43, 135 yd (123 m) natural white, 135 yd (123 m) dark brown #20 and 790 yd (719 m) rust #42.

WEFT: Same as the warp: 332 yd (302 m) rust. Textured cotton at 500 yd/lb (1000 m/kg). This is Cotton Clouds Aurora Cloud, available in 375 yd (341 m)/12 oz cones: 375 yd (341 m) white twisted with brown.

NOTIONS: Sewing thread.

E.P.I.: 20 (80/10 cm).

HEDDLE: 10-dent (40/10), threaded with doubled yarn (10 working ends per inch or 40/10 cm).

WIDTH IN HEDDLE: 15" (37.5 cm).

TOTAL WARP ENDS: 300.

WARP LENGTH: 4 yd (3.6 m), which includes take-up, shrinkage, and 18" (45 cm) loom waste.

THREADING: Because the heddle will be threaded with double strands, use this shortcut. Do not cut the end loops near the warp cross. Thread each loop through a hole or slot in the heddle and hook it onto the back beam. The loop makes a double strand. After threading all the loops, wind the warp onto the back beam and tie the ends to the cloth beam.

WEFT ROWS PER INCH: 15 (60/10 cm).

TAKE-UP & SHRINKAGE: 15% in width and 10% in length.

WEAVING: Weave 1¼" (3 cm) for hem with single strand of rust, weave 18" (45 cm) alternating rows of rust and textured cotton, weave 1¼" (3 cm) hem with rust. Measurements are with the tension relaxed. Weave a shot of contrasting yarn as a cutting mark between placemats.

FINISHING: Machine stitch on each side of the cutting mark and cut apart placemats. Turn under ¼" (5 mm), then ½" (10 mm), and hem by hand to the first textured row. Machine wash on gentle cycle and dry in dryer. Iron lightly. □

WARP COLOR ORDER:

begin ▶

Orange	24			24 =	48
Natural		16		16 =	32
Dark Brown			16	16 =	32
Rust			188	=	188
				TOTAL ENDS =	**300**

Warp stripes

Plain weave can be varied with color. The simplest color effect comes from making a warp of one color and crossing it with a weft of another color. From that point, the possibilities rapidly multiply.

One of the easiest ways to get variety into your weaving is to put stripes in the warp. You can cross your warp stripes with one color of weft, or you can weave with several colors and produce a plaid.

Plaids can be woven in many ways. You can use the same color order in the weft as in the warp. You can also follow the same sequence but use different colors, use the same colors in a different sequence, or change both colors and sequence. Designing plaids can be as simple or as complex as you want it to be.

Warping methods for stripes

When it's time to put warp stripes on your loom, some modifications of your warping technique will help. If you measure the warp ends in the order you want them on the loom, they will go onto the loom as easily as a solid color warp.

Before you start a project with warp stripes, study your design and decide which of the following ways will work best. The width of the stripes and the number of color changes will determine the method you choose.

Wide stripes. Measure the number of warp ends required for the first stripe. When it's time to change colors, cut off the first color just past one of the end pegs and tie on the new color.

Repeat as necessary for your design.

Alternating colors. Measure the two colors together, carrying a strand of each together around the pegs. When you are ready to pull the loops through the heddle, two loops (one of each color) will come off the cross at a time. Separate these loops and pull them through adjoining slots. The loops will alternate colors across the heddle.

After you have wound the warp onto the back beam and have cut the end loops at the front of the loom, you will be ready to thread the holes of the heddle. If you want two-thread stripes, simply thread as you would for a one-color warp.

If you want to alternate single threads, you'll have to reposition three out of every four warp ends to produce the correct color order, but the process will go quickly. Thread all the warp ends

of one color in the slots and all those of the other color in the holes.

Random or graduating stripes. When color changes occur frequently, it becomes tedious to have to cut and tie on a new color each time. Instead, make a separate warp chain for each color.

If all of your stripes will have even numbers of warp ends, you can thread the loops through the heddle in the order in which you want them, and then proceed as usual.

If some of your stripes will have odd numbers of warp ends, cut the loops at the end where the cross was made *before* you start to thread the heddle. Thread the single warp ends through the heddle, placing them in the holes and slots wherever you want them. Remember to center the warp in the heddle, and repeat with each warp chain until all the slots and holes in the desired width are filled.

With this method, you won't have loops to hook on the teeth on the back beam. Let the cut ends of the warp hang behind the heddle until you have finished threading. Gather up ½-inch (1.25 cm) sections of warp and straighten them out so the cut ends are even. Tie an overhand knot close to the ends of each bundle, making sure that the end of each warp thread is caught in the knot. Also check to be sure the knots are all the same distance from the ends of the bundles. Slip each bundle over the teeth on the back beam as you did the loops, or slip the dowel rod through the centers of the bundles and then attach it to the extension cords. Proceed with warping as usual.

This method allows you to spontaneously design stripes; it's also a good way to put on a warp where the colors blend subtly from one to another and don't produce a strongly striped effect.

Keeping track of your ideas

When you get ideas for warp stripes or weft sequences, you don't have to keep them in your head until you transfer them to the loom. A **draft** is the written form of a weave plan.

Across the top of the draft are two rows of squares to keep track of your warp. One row represents the slot threads and the other represents the hole threads.

You can use this section to plan the placement of colors in the warp. For example, if you want a fabric with wide stripes in two colors on the edges which blend into each other through a series of increasingly narrow stripes in the middle you can plot the placement of each warp color across the width.

If you will be designing weft sequences, you'll put two columns down the righthand side to represent them. One column stands for the up shed and one for the down shed.

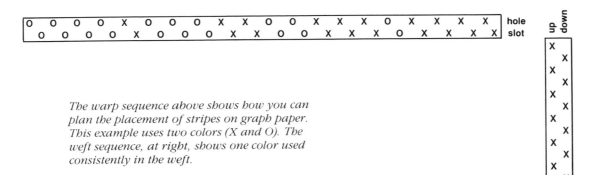

The warp sequence above shows how you can plan the placement of stripes on graph paper. This example uses two colors (X and O). The weft sequence, at right, shows one color used consistently in the weft.

This is the same warp sequence. The weft plan at right repeats the same sequence, to create a plaid effect.

Mohair Shawl

Designed by Dixie Straight

FABRIC DESCRIPTION: Plain weave.

FINISHED DIMENSIONS: 18″ (45 cm) wide × 72″ (180 cm) long, plus 6″ (15 cm) fringe on each end.

WARP & WEFT: 78% mohair/13% wool/8% nylon at 960 yd/lb (1920 m/kg). This is Brushed Mohair NS-MB from Ironstone Warehouse: 425 yd (387 m) Natural #88, 75 yd (69 m) Sea Mist #333.

E.P.I.: 6 (24/10 cm).

HEDDLE: 12-dent (48/10) threaded for half-density (see page 99).

WIDTH IN HEDDLE: 20″ (50 cm).

TOTAL WARP ENDS: 120.

WARP LENGTH: 2½ yds (225 cm), which includes take-up, shrinkage, and 18″ (45 cm) loom waste.

WEFT ROWS PER INCH: 5.

THREADING: Measure and warp the loom in this sequence—25 ends Natural, 15 ends Sea Mist, 20 ends Natural, 10 ends Sea Mist, 20 ends Natural, 5 ends Sea Mist, 25 ends Natural.

WEAVING: Tie on allowing 8″ (20 cm) for fringe. With Natural, weave 4 rows beating firmly. Weave 80″ (200 cm) beating regularly, then finish with 4 rows beaten firmly. Cut warp at the back beam and carefully remove reed. Untie knots at the front of the loom.

FINISHING: At each end of the shawl, make twisted fringe by twisting 2 groups of 3 warps clockwise and then twisting them together in the opposite direction and securing with a knot (see page 104). To keep the fringe from tangling during washing, gather the fringe on one end of the shawl and wind a rubber band around the tips. Repeat on the other end. Hand wash in warm water and mild soap. Rinse using fabric softener. Remove the rubber bands; carefully roll the shawl in a towel to remove moisture. Dry flat. Lightly press the shawl with an iron and a pressing cloth, straightening the fringe and trimming it to 6″ (15 cm). □

An elegant mohair shawl that's a breeze to weave—two colors of stripes in the warp, and one color in the weft.

Color-and-weave effects

When a sequence of light and dark ends in the warp is crossed with a sequence of light and dark weft picks, the resulting patterns are called **color-and-weave effects.** Color-and-weave effects are closely related to plaids, although the stripes from which they are developed are often very narrow. Many color-and-weave patterns can be created from only two colors, although with three or more colors the possibilities increase. The visual effect created by color-and-weave patterns looks far more complex than its simple weave structure.

The weft sequence can be the same as or different from the warp sequence. The visual pattern is quite distinct from the weave structure. It's not the choice of colors but the interaction between two (or more) colors that makes these patterns.

A sampler will let you see how a wide variety of color-and-weave patterns can be produced. The visibility of these color-and-weave patterns depends on the contrast between light and dark. Black and white provide the greatest contrast, but any colors can be used. If there is little contrast, the patterns will be subtle, or perhaps very hard to see.

Many exciting ideas can be developed from color-and-weave patterns. For variety, a weft yarn can be slightly different in color than its corresponding warp color. For example, if the warps are red and white, try wefts in maroon and cream. The red and maroon should have approximately the same value, or darkness, just as the white and cream have about the same lightness. The resulting fabric will have more depth than one which uses only two colors. Additional colors can also be introduced. Several patterns can be combined in one piece; a sampler will help you figure out which threading sequences make attractive patterns with which weft sequences.

While the dark/light sequences provide a good understanding of how color-and-weave works, the ideas behind them can be applied to many different kinds of yarn. You can use thick and thin yarns, shiny and dull ones, hairy and slick, smooth and textured. You could work with close colors or slightly different naturals to produce a very subtle or tone-on-tone effect.

Color-and-weave effects can be used with different colors, textures, or weights of yarn. The patterns on the left were produced by using warp sequences like those developed in the sampler (righthand page) along with wider stripes and repeating the sequences in the weft. The swatches on the right were designed by using thick and thin yarns in similar colors in overall patterns like those developed in each section of the sampler.

SAMPLERS

Weave a sampler to experiment with color blending, color sequences (color-and-weave), or groupings or spacings of warp and weft threads. Divide the warp into several sections and thread each in a different sequence. One or more warp ends of a contrasting color can divide each section from the next. Include a section of plain threading at each edge.

When you weave, use the same sequence in the weft as in the warp. If the first section of warp is threaded in alternating black and white threads, the first weft section will also alternate black and white threads. As each of the weft sections crosses the warp, one section will be symmetrical because the weft and warp sequences will be the same. The other sections will be surprises.

Each section should be 3 to 4 inches (7.5 to 10 cm) wide and 3 to 4 inches (7.5 to 10 cm) long, so you'll be able to see what's happening. You'll get lots of new ideas through this kind of experimenting. Wash and press the sampler before you make

any judgments about the different sections.

To use a sampler effectively, you need to study each square by itself. There is so much going on in the whole sampler that you need to isolate one section at a time to evaluate it. Cut a square out of one corner of two pieces of lightweight cardboard, making two L-shaped frame sections. Used together, these pieces can be adjusted to make windows of different sizes. When placed over one of the squares, the window frame isolates that pattern. The sampler can also be folded so you can see how several combinations look side by side.

The sampler pictured here shows color-and-weave effects. The sections were woven using weft ends in the same order as they appear in the warp. You can see from the draft that each square explores a different sequence of light and dark warps. The weft is woven in the same color order. These light/dark sequences are classic combinations; you can experiment with more light/dark sequences of your own.

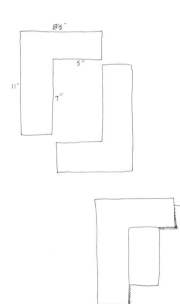

A sampler is the best way to explore color-and-weave effects. The sections moving diagonally up from the lower righthand corner demonstrate what happens when warp and weft follow the same sequences. The asymmetrical patterns can be equally fascinating.

B = black
W = white
★ = heliotrope

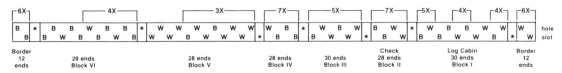

This sampler was woven at 10 E.P.I. in a two-ply wool at 1650 yd/lb (3300 m/kg). This is Novi-wool by Novitex, in white #101, black #36, and heliotrope #3. Warp ends: 173 in blocks I-VI, 24 in borders, 7 to divide blocks = 204 total (98 black, 99 white, 7 heliotrope). The weft sequence follows that used in the warp.

LOG CABIN EFFECT

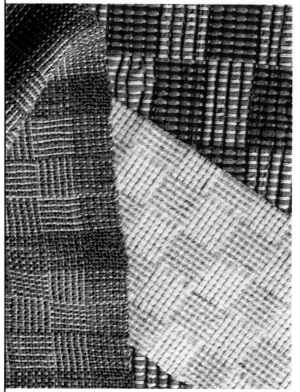

Log cabin is the name of one popular color-and-weave effect. You can see the basic idea in the first section (lower righthand corner) of the color-and-weave sampler. Log cabin is designed with two **blocks,** or threading repeats. One consists of light threads in the holes and dark threads in the slots, and the other consists of dark threads in the holes and light threads in the slots. The pattern develops as these blocks are alternated across the warp and as the weft sequences similarly alternate.

When the weft sequence is the same as the warp sequence, very fine vertical and horizontal stripes are formed. The direction of the stripes in each section can be changed by reversing the color order in the weft.

The overall look of log cabin depends on the colors used at the switching point between blocks. The blocks can be made any size; they don't always have to be square. Try narrow and wide blocks.

Log cabin, like all the color-and-weave effects, can be infinitely varied by your choice of yarns.

The swatch on the left alternates log cabin sections with plain blue stripes in both warp and weft. The fabric on the upper right alternates thick (rag) and thin wefts on a red-and-white log cabin warp. The white swatch blends thick and thin, shiny and matte, textured and smooth yarns in a subtle range of colors.

In the lefthand swatch, the shift between blocks, or threading repeats, is made by putting two light warps together. In the center swatch, the switch is made by putting two dark warps together; this gives an effect of weft stripes interweaving with warp stripes. In the righthand swatch, the blocks shift alternately: the first switch is made by putting two dark warps together, while the second one places two light warps together. This same pattern appears in the log cabin section of the color-and-weave sampler.

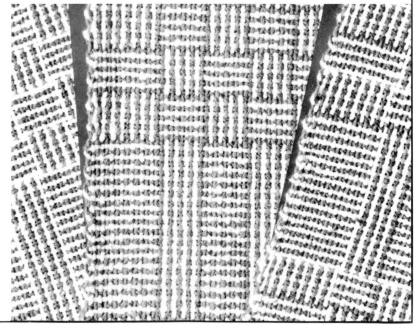

Weft-emphasis and Weft-faced Fabrics

Weft-emphasis fabrics are those in which the weft tends to cover up most of the warp. The warp is spaced more widely than it would be for a balanced weave so the weft is beaten down over it more. This kind of weaving gives you an opportunity to weave with warp yarns that are otherwise too fine for use with a single rigid heddle. For example, a yarn that should be woven at 15 EPI for a balanced weave can be threaded in a 12-dent heddle to achieve the wider spacing of a weft-emphasis fabric.

In fabric of this type the weft is often heavier than the warp. This may or may not mean there are more weft rows per inch than warps per inch; the number of picks per inch depends on the contrast in size between warp and weft. A fine warp set at 12 EPI may only take 6 rows of a thick weft. The weft will dominate because it is heavier.

With this type of weaving, you can explore wefts other than yarns. Try cloth strips, unspun wool fleece, leather strips, and other unconventional materials.

A **weft-faced** plain weave is one in which the weft *completely* covers the warp. The warp is completely covered by the weft. Imagine a Navajo rug: it is a weft-faced fabric. The weft is laid loosely in the shed so it can curve over and under the warp, which remains straight. Weft-faced fabrics are slower to weave than balanced weaves; however, since only the weft shows, the color combinations are easier to plan. The weft colors are not modified by the color of the warp, as they are in balanced weave, where warp and weft colors visually blend in the finished fabric.

Yarns

The warp yarn for a weft-faced weave should be a smooth, strong, plied yarn. Popular warp yarns for weft-faced weaves are 8/4 cotton rug warp and 8/4 linen rug warp. The weft is usually quite a bit thicker and softer than the warp. The ideal weft is a soft, lofty wool yarn that will curve easily as it is beaten down over the warp. Don't limit yourself to wool, however. Try other types of yarns; they might give interesting effects.

Generally a weft-faced weave has a lot of body. Since the weft material is emphasized, the fabric will be stiffer in the weft direction, which

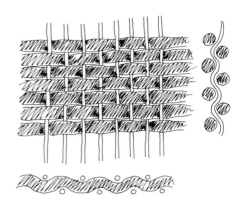

A weft-emphasis fabric.

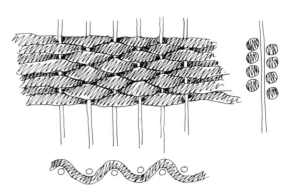

A weft-faced fabric.

is a bonus in textiles that need to lie or hang flat, such as runners, table mats, and rugs. The combination of a linen warp and a dense, coarse wool weft tightly beaten down will produce a stiff fabric. This textile will be durable and will keep its shape. A softer weft yarn will make a more flexible fabric. For vests and jackets, a weft-faced weave with a drapable hand can be made by using a smooth, fine, tightly twisted wool (like 12/3 Oregon Worsted Nehalem) for the warp, with a softly spun wool weft beaten down so it just covers the warp.

Sett

For a weft-faced weave, the warp must be spaced far enough apart to allow the weft yarns to slide down and completely cover the warp.

Figuring a sett for weft-faced weaving takes some trial-and-error experimenting. The best thing to do is try the combination of warp and weft and see if they give the effect you want. Try setts of 6 or 8 rather than finer setts.

A rough guideline for weft-faced setts can be obtained through a modification of the ruler-wrapping technique. Hold together one strand

Tote Bags

Designed by Betty Davenport

FABRIC DESCRIPTION: Weft-faced plain weave with color effects and rows of 3-thread floats.

FINISHED DIMENSIONS: Each bag is 13" (32.5 cm) square with 35" (87.5 cm) handles.

WARP: 8/4 cotton carpet warp at 1600 yd/lb (3200 m/kg): 354 yd (322 m) brown.

WEFT: Pattern—2 ply wool at 1040 yd/lb (2080 m/kg). This is Artissa from Miranda Imports, available in 525 yd (478 m)/8 oz skeins: 100 yd (91 m) Wine, 65 yd (59 m) each of Terra, Gris, and Suelo. **Background**—2-ply wool at 1400 yd/lb (2800 m/kg). This is Sportweight Green Pastures Perendale from The Yarnery: 300 yd (273 m) each of Charcoal and Scots Mist. (SN-2 from Glimåkra Looms 'n Yarns at 1560 yd/lb [3120 m/kg] could be substituted for the Perendale: use charcoal #1104 and beige #2).

E.P.I.: 10 (40/10 cm).

HEDDLE: 10-dent (40/10).

WIDTH IN HEDDLE: 13½" (33.75 cm).

TOTAL WARP ENDS: 135.

WARP LENGTH: 2½ yd (2.25 m), which includes take-up, shrinkage, and 18" (45 cm) loom waste.

THREADING: Start and end threading in holes of the heddle.

WEFT ROWS PER INCH: 30 (120/10 cm).

TAKE-UP & SHRINKAGE: 4% in width and 1% in length.

WEAVING: Beige bag—weave 1½" (3.75 cm) to be turned under for a hem, 13½" (33.75 cm) to the fold at the bottom, another 13½" (33.75 cm), and 1½" (3.75 cm) for a hem. Use the color patterns described below within the 13½" (33.75 cm) sections. Each color effect pattern is separated from the next by 1¼" (3 cm) beige. **Charcoal bag**—weave color pattern variations as above, and use weft float patterns and variations, at random and with various colors.

STRAPS: Make 30 ends 1½ yds (135 cm) long, using mostly the main weft color but adding some stripes in contrasting colors. Double the ends in a 10-dent (40/10) heddle so that the strap will be 1½" (3.75 cm) wide. Use a single strand of the main color for weft.

FINISHING: Steam well, taking care not to touch the fabric with the iron.

ASSEMBLY: Beige bag—make overhand knots with pairs of warps. Fold the bag in half and sew the selvedges together by overcasting them with a doubled strand of beige. Turn down the hem at the top and hand hem. Attach the strap by tucking about 1" (2.5 cm) of each end inside the bag and stitching by hand. **Charcoal bag**—fold bag in half and close the side seam by knotting warps from each end together. Sew the bottom edge closed by overcasting the selvedges with a doubled strand of charcoal. Attach the strap the same way as in the beige bag. □

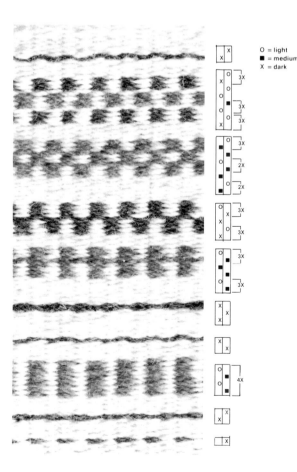

O = light
■ = medium
X = dark

Left: Color patterns in weft-faced plain weave are simple, but allow infinite variety. The weft plan indicates the pattern rows, but does not include the white background that appears between the patterns.

Right: If you supplement weft-faced patterns with floats, you can do even more. The short floats are done on a 1 up/1 down pick-up; the long floats result from a 1 up/2 down sequence. Floats can be made with either the background or the contrasting color; see page 45.

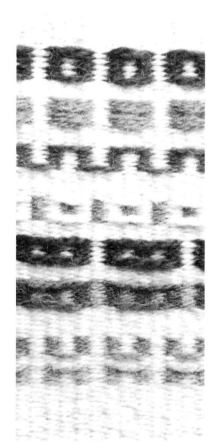

Weaving these bags will give you an opportunity to experiment with weft-faced patterning. After they're completed, they'll sturdily carry books, small parcels, or knitting.

Band 1

Band 3

Warp-faced bands are fun to design, and can be used for straps and belts or joined into wider fabrics.

Warp-faced bands

The **beige and tan band** is based on the log cabin threading idea. The variations in thickness of the crosswise stripes result from the use of two wefts, one thick and one thin. This 100% wool band was woven with 12/3 worsted wool at 2160 yd/lb (4325 m/kg).

The **blue, white, and silver band** uses the log cabin idea—alternating light and dark threads—to make two areas in which warp floats can be picked up to supplement the design. Bands are a good way to use miscellaneous yarns. This cotton band is made from 5/2 pearl cotton at 2100 yd/lb (4200 m/kg) in white, 8/2 pearl cotton at 3400 yd/lb (6840 m/kg) used double in blue, and metallic sewing machine thread used double in silver.

The **ivory, purple, and red band** derives its texture from the occasional use of doubled strands of a slubby yarn against a background of smooth yarns. The beige and green strands are 8/4 cotton carpet warp at 1600 yd/lb (3200 m/kg). The red and purple "flowers" are two-ply slub cotton at 1100 yd/lb (2200 m/kg).

The **white, red, brown, and black band** is 10/2 linen at 1350 yd/lb (2700 m/kg).

The **blue and red band** uses alternating colors to produce yet another type of design. This is 3/2 pearl cotton at 1260 yd/lb (2520 m/kg).

Band 1

		8 ×		8 ×		8 ×		8 ×		8 ×		
tan	6	1		1		1		1			1	6
beige		1		1		1		1		1		
blue			2				2					
ochre				2					2			

Band 2

ivory	4	3	4	4	3	4
light green	1					
red			3		3	
purple			3			

Band 3

						floats 5 ×		floats 5 ×				
light blue			2	2		1		1		2	2	
blue	4	4			2				2		4	4
white		5		3	2	1	3	1	2	3		5
silver	2		1					1			2	

Band 4

		4 ×							4 ×		
white	4		1	4	2	2	2	4		1	4
red		1	1	2				2		1	1
brown				2		3	2				
black					2		2				

Band 5

		6 ×		6 ×		6 ×		6 ×		
light blue	6	1							1	6
med. blue				1	6	1				
burgundy	1	6	1							
red							1	6	1	

48

Warp-emphasis and Warp-faced Fabrics

A **warp-emphasis** fabric is one in which the warp shows more than the weft. The warp yarns are set more closely than for a balanced weave. Warp emphasis is one way to retain the color relationships in warp stripes with less influence from the weft color. A **warp-faced** weave is the extreme of warp emphasis, since *only* the warp shows. The weft appears only at the edges, where it turns to enter the next shed.

As versatile as the rigid heddle loom is, it cannot handle a wide variety of warp-emphasis and warp-faced fabrics. You can make a warp-emphasis fabric by selecting as large a yarn as will fit *easily* through the holes in your heddle (remember, you'll have to move the heddle back and forth over the warp). A yarn that would normally be set at 8 EPI for a balanced weave can be threaded into a 10-dent (40/10) heddle and the resulting fabric will emphasize the warp yarns somewhat. However, the same yarn would probably be too heavy to fit through the holes of a 12-dent (48/10) heddle. In a warp-faced fabric the warp ends must be very close together, which, as we have noted, is not possible on the rigid heddle because of the restricted spacing of the holes and slots.

Despite these restrictions, narrow warp-faced bands can be woven on the rigid heddle loom. You use the heddle only to change the sheds, not to beat, and draw the warps in close together with the weft as you weave.

Because the warp ends are pulled in, there's a lot of stress on the outside warp ends and a 3-inch (10 cm) band is about the widest you should plan on weaving on your rigid heddle loom. Bands can be put to many uses. You can make a belt to complement a handwoven top, trim for the edge of a vest, or a strap for a bag.

Yarns

There will be a lot of friction on the yarns when you change sheds, especially on the edge yarns. You'll find that strong, smooth, and well twisted yarns are easiest to work with.

The weft yarn can be the same size as the warp, or finer, or heavier. Its weight will affect the finished appearance of your band, although it will show only at the selvedges. If you choose a color the same as that of the edge warp ends, it won't be very noticeable. Interesting effects

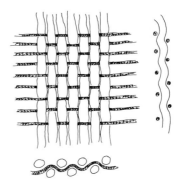

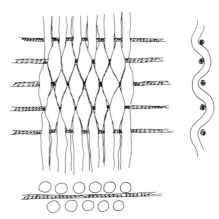

A warp-emphasis fabric.

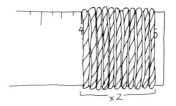

A warp-faced fabric.

happen in some patterns when a very fine and a very heavy weft are alternated.

Sett

To determine the approximate number of warps which will appear in 1 inch (2.5 cm) of a finished warp-faced band, wind the warp yarn around a ruler for an inch (2.5 cm). Count the number of turns and double it. You won't use this number to determine which heddle to use, since the heddle will only form the sheds, but you will use it to figure out how many warp ends you need. When you weave your band, you may find that it is a little narrower than you intended, depending on how tightly you pull the weft into place.

For a warp-faced sett, multiply the number of wraps in 1 inch by 2 (or the number in 5 cm by 4).

Designing

Since only the warp shows, all the color effects will be in the warp yarns. Warp-faced designs use the same principles as weft-faced designs; the sequence of colors forms the patterns. Look at the sampler in the section on weft-faced weaving. Turn it 90 degrees and imagine that the weft has become the warp. The sequences of warp colors for the basic patterns are:

1. Dotted line—one warp of contrasting color
2. Solid wavy line—two warps of contrasting
3. Solid bumpy line—three warps of contrasting color
4. Horizontal bar—alternate two colors for desired width of bar
5. Horizontal bar with center stripe—odd number of contrasting color warps in center
6. Horizontal bars alternated—even number of contrasting color warps in center

You can combine these patterns with solid stripes for an unlimited number of band designs. Introduce more colors. Repeat units of the last pattern several times and weave with alternating heavy and fine wefts to produce a log cabin-type design.

Sampling shortcuts

With a weft-faced project, you can design as you go, but when you are doing a warp-faced fabric the planning must be done in advance. It's always worthwhile to do a sample before investing a lot of time and yarn in a finished piece that may not be what you wanted. It is especially important to try different possibilities ahead of time if you are making a band to coordinate with something else. The colors may not look as you thought they would, the width may be wrong, or the design may turn out to be incompatible with the piece you want it to complement. Once you've warped the loom, it is difficult to make changes. But there are several quick ways to make samples, both with yarn and on paper.

Warp-faced bands can be designed on a *weft-faced* warp, where it's simple to experiment with color and pattern. Wind a quick sample warp around the pegs of a rigid heddle loom that has toothed beams, or use the sampling method on page 91 to adapt your dowel-rod loom for fast samples. You can also wind a warp around a picture frame or piece of heavy cardboard. The sample warp can be just 2 or 3 inches (5 to 7.5 cm) wide. Since the heddle is not used, form one

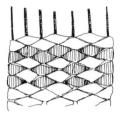
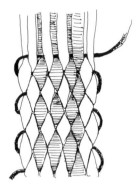

Above, *a band has been designed on a weft-faced warp.* Right, *the sequence of wefts has been rotated 90 degrees and becomes a sequence of warps.*

shed by inserting a pick-up stick to lift every other thread. This stick can stay in place. Form the other shed by picking up the opposite threads with a needle or another pick-up stick; this shed will have to be picked each time.

In warp-faced weaving, the heddle is used only to change sheds. A narrow-edged belt shuttle carries the weft and is used as a beater. The narrow width of the band is established when you tie the warps to the front dowel or beam. Even width can be gauged with a device (page 53) made from toothpicks and paper.

For finer yarns, such as pearl cotton or cotton rug warp, wind your sample at 8 or 10 EPI. For heavier yarns, such as a medium-weight wool, use 5 EPI.

Review some of the basic patterns by weaving a small sampler for future reference. You have seen how the same light/dark alternations you used in the weft-faced fabric can be applied to warp-faced designs. Use two contrasting colors, one for the background and one for the pattern. You will need only small amounts of weft yarn, cut into 18-inch (45 cm) lengths or made into small butterflies. Repeat each pattern several times, and weave at least six shots of background color between pattern sections. Be sure the weft covers the warp!

When you have your sampler, you can design a band because you will be able to see a variety of patterns. If you play with color, sequence, and proportion on a weft-faced fabric, you will get an accurate idea of how wide the equivalent warp-faced band will be. Make several combinations, in different sets of colors. Separate each sample band from the next one with a 1-inch (1.25 cm) strip of heavy paper, so you can see it without being confused by its neighbors. If you don't like what you're seeing, you can pull it out and try something else.

When you are satisfied with the pattern and color balance, rotate your sample a quarter-turn

so the weft represents the warp, and count the number of "ends" of each color (formerly weft picks). Then you can chart the sequence of colors and warp your loom to match. Make your warp longer than you think you might need—you can lose up to 30 percent of the length in take-up, depending on the thickness of your weft.

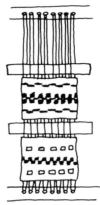

You can also design warp-faced bands on graph paper, using colored pencils to keep track of the patterns. This method doesn't give any idea of scale or of the width of the woven band, and you'll have to guess how the actual yarn colors will work together, but can be worked out quickly when you've had a little experience with the patterns. Only two lines on the graph paper are needed to represent the warp ends,

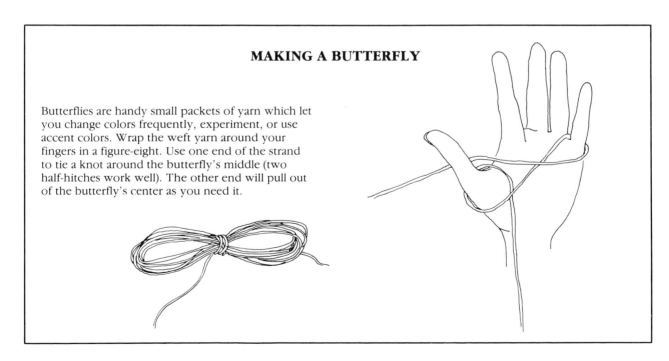

MAKING A BUTTERFLY

Butterflies are handy small packets of yarn which let you change colors frequently, experiment, or use accent colors. Wrap the weft yarn around your fingers in a figure-eight. Use one end of the strand to tie a knot around the butterfly's middle (two half-hitches work well). The other end will pull out of the butterfly's center as you need it.

one for the slot threads and the other for the hole threads. Repeat each design at least three times vertically on the graph paper to get the effect of the pattern.

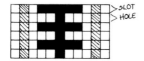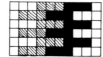

Warping

Use the heddle with the smallest possible spacing to minimize the difference between the width of the woven piece and the spread of the warp in the heddle. If a 1-inch (2.5 cm) band has 40 warp ends, the spread in the heddle will be 4 inches (10 cm) if they are threaded in a 10-dent (40/10) heddle or 3¼ inches (8 cm) in a 12-dent (48/10) heddle. The narrower the warp is in the heddle, the more even the tension will be.

Warp the loom as usual, except for tying onto the front beam. At this point the warp must be gathered to the width of the planned weaving. Tie groups of warp ends in overhand knots and lash the groups to the front beam.

Weaving

Since the weaving is narrower than the warp's width in the heddle, the heddle serves only to change sheds and not for beating. Use a bevel-edged weaving sword, a stick shuttle, a table knife, or a small wooden ruler as a beater—the

ruler will help you check the width of your band. Open the shed and pass the weft, leaving a 3-inch (7.5 cm) tail sticking out. Change the shed, beating sharply with the sword. Lay both the tail and the weft into this next shed; the excess can be trimmed off later. Pull on both tail and weft to adjust the weaving to the desired width. Pass the weft again, change sheds, beat, and adjust the weft. Always beat after the shed has been changed, and then adjust the weft to make a neat selvedge. With each weft shot, the tension on the warp will become a fraction tighter. Roll the warp forward frequently so the tension remains uniform.

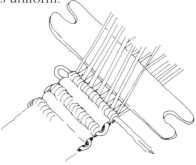

Change sheds and beat, then pull the weft to snug the loop at the selvedge.

The challenge in weaving narrow bands is to maintain an even width. You can check your width by making a gauge. After you have woven about an inch (2-3 cm), measure the width of your band. Cut a piece of paper 2 inches (5 cm) longer and 1 inch (2.5 cm) wider than the band. Fold it in half, and cut a window out of the

---

LASHING ON

Lashing on can be used to gather the warp ends to a narrow width for band weaving or to minimize loom waste. You do not have to place the heddle in the up position while you lash groups of warp onto the cloth beam; the warp layers will become equal in tension with the first few rows of weft, which will be woven as usual with scrap yarn.

Attach a long strand of a strong, smooth cord (the lashing cord) to one end of the dowel rod or the toothed beam, even with one edge of your weaving width. If you will be weaving a narrow band, this edge will establish the drawing-in of the warp to the width of the finished band. Pick up the first group of warp ends and loop the lashing cord through the opening between the slot and hole threads (the middle of the group). Take the free end of the cord around the dowel or a tooth, pull on it until the group comes close to the dowel or teeth,

then go through the middle of the next group. Continue across the warp. At the opposite edge of the warp width, again tie the lashing cord to the dowel or warp beam.

Go back and lift each group in sequence, evening out any slack in the cord. Adjust small discrepancies in tension by rolling or twisting the dowel or beam back and forth a few times.

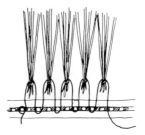

folded edge of the paper to match the band's width. Place the gauge under the band so the band rests in the opening. Slide a toothpick under the folded edge of the paper and tape the edge closed. The gauge will hang conveniently on the band and you can check your width after every few shots.

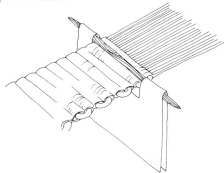

You can neatly secure the final end of your weft with another trick. On the next to the last shot at the end of your band, lay a large needle in the shed along with the weft yarn with its point in the same direction the weft is headed. Change the shed, beat, pass the weft again, trim the weft yarn to about four inches (10 cm), and thread the end through the needle. Pull the needle and the weft through the second-to-last shed and clip off the excess weft.

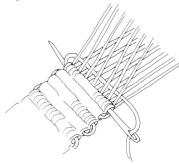

Weave a large-eyed needle into the second-to-the-last shed and then use it to hide the final weft tail.

After you trim the fringe, the warp ends may be left as they are or you can finish them with the methods described in "In the End." Twisting or braiding the ends works especially well.

Float patterns

Bolder patterns can be made on warp-faced bands if you pick up warp floats in the sections which have a basic pattern of horizontal stripes. These are the areas where light and dark warps alternate. Some of these patterns repeat regularly and can be made with the technique you have already used, where the pick-up is made behind the heddle using the slot warps only. Again, the stick can stay in place and be used repeatedly.

Warp floats can be picked up in pairs or singly. You can work out simple designs which combine floats with the horizontal bar pattern, including boxes, "I"s, "H"s, and zigzags.

Place the heddle in the down shed position and pick up only the slot warps you want to use in the float pattern. The weaving sequence is:
(1) Down shed
(2) Up shed, pattern stick forward
(3) Down shed
(4) Up shed.
Experiment with the effects which occur when you alternate a heavy weft with a finer weft.

The warp-faced pattern on the lefthand edge of this photo comes from alternating the background (white) with the pattern color (blue). You can do pick-up patterns on areas which are threaded this way, as shown at the bottom righthand corner. Other pattern possibilities, from top to bottom, come from: one strand of contrasting color, two strands of contrasting color, three strands of contrasting color, alternating light and dark/two strands dark/alternating light and dark, alternating light and dark/alternating dark and light. Samples were woven with both lightweight wefts, seen on the right of the photograph, and heavyweight wefts, seen as the bands move left.

Hand-controlled Weaves

There are lots of ways to add interest to plain weave fabrics beyond the pick-up patterning we've already talked about. You can weave in pattern areas using extra weft yarns, or create lacy effects by manipulating warps and wefts in different ways. Tapestry, which is a whole area of study in itself, is briefly included here, since it is a weft-faced plain weave in which areas of weft color are built up to make intricate designs.

None of these techniques can be duplicated by machines, so you can use them to weave truly one-of-a-kind fabrics.

Open Weaves

With your loom threaded to plain weave and a pick-up stick, you can weave lace-like fabrics. In the open weaves, either the warps or wefts are deflected or grouped to make an open, airy fabric that is still stable. The open weaves can be used as border rows, or overall patterns, or in small areas.

Leno

Leno weaves create very delicate and lacy fabrics. Leno is worked by twisting or crossing the warp threads and then holding them in that position with the weft.

You should keep your warp tension just slightly looser than usual when working rows of leno, to allow a little slack for crossing the warps. The shed through which you put the weft will be formed by a pick-up stick, so it won't be large: use a narrow stick shuttle without too much yarn wound onto it. Leno areas tend to draw in, so it's important to leave sufficient weft ease in the leno sheds. There won't be much room to lay the weft in at an angle, but you can bubble it a little bit, as you did for the weft-faced fabrics, and be sure not to pull it tightly into position.

Follow each step carefully. Lenos weave up more quickly than you may think from reading the directions. You will find that only two weft shots produce about ½ inch (1.25 cm) of pattern.

The trick in leno is figuring out which direction to cross the warps. To weave the basic 1/1 or single leno, where one warp crosses another, begin by opening a *new* shed. You can make the crossings in either shed. You'll work with pairs of warps, and each pair consists of a warp end in the upper layer and the warp end that lies next to it in the lower layer. Work with the warps by twos, beginning at the selvedge from which you will start your crossing (the righthand selvedge for most weavers). The edge warp can be either up or down.

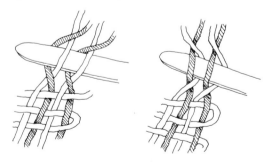

The only trick in leno is figuring out which direction to cross the warps. There are only two possibilities.

Looking at the first pair, determine in which direction the upper warp has to move in order to cross the lower warp. If the bottom warp lies to the left of the top warp, the top one will have to move to the left in order to cross it. If the bottom warp lies to the right, the top warp will have to move to the right to make the cross. If you move the top warp in the wrong direction, you won't get a twist. Once you've figured how to twist the first pair, all the other pairs on that row will twist in the same way.

In the first pair of warps, cross the top warp over the bottom warp. Slide the pick-up stick into the twist so it holds the warps in place. Repeat the twist with the second pair and slip the pick-up stick into place. As you make additional twists, keep the warps on the pick-up stick pulled to the side with the forefinger of your right hand. Isolate the next pair to be crossed with your left index finger. These hand movements will increase your accuracy later when you work more complex twists.

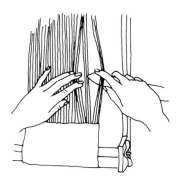

When you have finished the row, look at the warps on the pick-up stick to see if all the crosses look uniform. Mistakes can be corrected more easily before the weft has been passed through. When you are satisfied, turn the pick-up stick on edge to form the shed for the shuttle to pass through. Weave, then turn the pick-up stick flat again and use it to press the twists into place as tightly as possible. Slide the pick-up stick out. Then open the opposite shed with the rigid heddle, clear it by moving the heddle toward you, and pass the weft through this shed. Beat or press the weft down as tightly as possible.

These two rows—one with the pick-up stick, followed by one in the opposite shed—complete one row of leno. The threads will have returned to their original positions.

You can immediately weave another leno row, or you can weave several rows of plain weave before doing more twists. If you want a fabric with good body, a single pattern row should be no more than ½ inch (1.25 cm) high if the warp is at 10 EPI (40/10).

Once you know how to determine the direction in which to make the twists, you can work leno in either plain weave shed or at any place across the warp—it doesn't need to cover the full width.

After you finish a leno piece, lay it on an ironing board, straighten its selvedges, and press it with a steam iron. A wall hanging will need only this pressing. Utilitarian items should be washed gently by hand.

You can vary leno in a lot of ways. Double leno, or 2/2, is larger, more defined, and works up faster. To do it, cross two warps from the top layer over two warps in the bottom layer. Larger lenos, crossing 3/3 or 4/4, can be made but tend to be practical only in special decorative circumstances. After you are very comfortable with twisting the ends, you could work 1/1 leno in the upper shed only or 2/2 leno on a closed shed. Leno worked on a closed shed produces a sharper, less delicate design. If you are intrigued by leno, you can find other variations in the resource books listed in the appendix.

 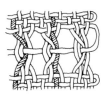

1/1 leno   *2/2 leno*

Brooks bouquet

The "bouquets" in this technique are formed when the weft wraps around and cinches up groups of warp ends. You can tell if you are looking at Brooks bouquet because of the crosshair-like weft yarns connecting the "bouquets." Consecutive rows make oval shapes.

Start by opening a new shed with the shuttle on the right side. Put the shuttle through the shed under four top warps, bring it out and to the right again around the same four warps, then insert the shuttle into the shed again under those four warps and under four more. Cinch the little bundle of warps up tight. Continue across, wrapping four warps into each group. On the last group, put the shuttle through the wrapping loop to make a knot which will keep the last bouquet from working loose.

Change the shed and weave at least three rows of plain weave before you work the next row of bouquets. Experiment by making the bouquets over different numbers of warps.

Try to keep all the weft loops at the same level. You can use the heddle to even up a line of bouquets, but it is difficult to beat them down very much. If you plan ahead, you can accent the bouquets by using a warp which is heavier or of a contrasting color on the edges of each group.

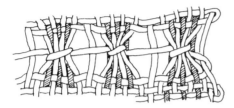

Brooks bouquet

Danish medallion

This technique became known in America as *Danish medallion* after it was discovered in an old weaving book from Denmark. It makes oval shapes by gathering together groups of *wefts*. The ovals show up best if a heavy yarn is used to make the outlines.

The linen fabric on the left is worked in leno, using the alternating format described on page 60. A variety of openwork techniques, combined with a weft float pattern, are used in the runner on the right, which is explained on pages 58-59.

Open a new shed. Cut a length of heavy yarn that is three times the width of the weaving and lay it into the shed loosely, leaving a 2-inch (5 cm) tail on the left edge. Weave ½ inch (1.25 cm) with your plain weave weft. *Don't* catch the heavy yarn in along the selvedge. Open a new shed, insert the heavy yarn for 1 inch (2.5 cm) and then bring it out of the shed to the surface. Poke a crochet hook through the fabric below the first heavy weft pick, catch a loop of the heavy weft and pull it through to the top. Take the end of the heavy weft through the loop to make a knot and pull it tight. Repeat at 1-inch (2.5 cm) intervals across the warp. On the left side, tuck the beginning tail in the shed and clip off the excess.

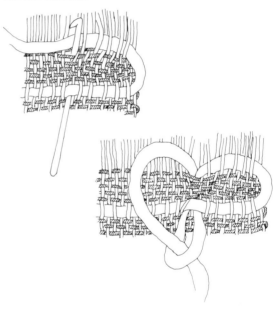

Danish medallion is worked in two steps, but goes quickly.

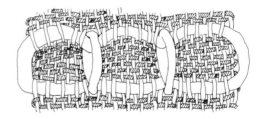

The medallions look most distinct if you tighten the heavy weft very snugly, to accent the oval shapes. However, you may want to leave the heavy weft looser for an airier effect. The amount of plain weave inside the oval relates to the width of the medallion; if you weave too much plain weave, it will be difficult to pull the medallion together.

Try making different sizes of medallions. Use a contrasting color for the heavy weft, or use a contrasting color for the plain weave inside.

Spanish lace

In Spanish lace, a technique used in traditional Spanish textiles, the weft zigzags back and forth as it works its way across the warp. The effect shows up best if a heavier weft yarn is used for the lace areas. Don't beat the weft in hard—in fact, it can lie quite loosely in the shed and make nice swirls.

Open a new shed. In the upper layer, count off the number of warps in 1 inch (2.5 cm) and insert the shuttle through the shed under that number of warps, bringing it out to the top surface. Change sheds, count the same number of warps in the new top layer and weave back 1 inch (2.5 cm) to the edge. Change sheds, count off the number of warps in 2 inches (5 cm) and weave over. Change sheds, weave back 1 inch (2.5 cm); change sheds and weave over 2 inches (5 cm); and so forth.

Spanish lace

Count the warps each time to make sure the groups are uniform. When you reach the opposite selvedge you will have finished three weft rows. Use a pick-up stick or a fork to press the wefts in place on each unit. At each turn, pull the weft snug so the open slit between the units becomes clearly defined. Spanish lace can be woven back from the left side to the right, or you can insert one row of plain weave and then work the lace from right to left again. The lace will look different, depending on the direction in which it is worked.

You can make each unit of the lace wider or narrower than this sample, and can weave back and forth more than three times in each unit. Experiment also with different weft yarns in the lace area.

Weaving hints

The trickiest part of doing any of these techniques is figuring out how to divide the warp into equal-sized groups. Count the warps in the upper layer and then decide approximately how many units you want to have across the width. If you will be alternating sections of pattern and plain weave, you will need to have an odd number of groups. Divide this number into the number of warps in the upper layer. If you wind up with "extra" warps, they can be divided equally and included in the outside sections.

Mark the unit divisions with pieces of yarn placed through the warp at the fell line. It's very important to include each upper warp's lower companion in the same group; check the beginning selvedge to see if the lower warp is to the left or right of the upper warp. Keep the upper/lower pairs together across the warp. The markers will indicate the boundaries within which you will work each technique or unit of a single technique. Mistakes in open weave areas most often occur when you transfer from one technique to another, and these reminders will help you make smooth transitions.

For formal occasions, what could be more satisfying than a linen runner you wove yourself? As you make it, you'll get practice with a variety of openwork techniques.

FABRIC DESCRIPTIONS: Linen plain weave background with openwork variations.

FINISHED DIMENSIONS: 17½″ (43.75 cm) wide × 39½″ (98.75 cm) long.

WARP: 10/2 linen at 1350 yd/lb (2700 m/kg). This is from Frederick J. Fawcett: 360 yds (328 m) natural.

WEFT: 5/1 slub linen at 1500 yd/lb (3000 m/kg). This is from Frederick J. Fawcett: 180 yd (164 m) pale yellow. Also a small amount of 25% linen/75% rayon at 1675 yd/lb (3353 m/kg). This is Nordica from Novitex, in #1116 burnt orange; use 4 strands as one.

E.P.I.: 12 (48/10 cm).

HEDDLE: 12-dent (48/10).

WIDTH IN HEDDLE: 18″ (45 cm).

TOTAL WARP ENDS: 216.

WARP LENGTH: 60″ (150 cm), which includes take-up, shrinkage, and 18″ (45 cm) loom waste.

WEFT ROWS PER INCH: 12 (48/10 cm).

WEAVING: With pale yellow, weave 5″ (12.5 cm) plain weave, followed by one row of 2/2 leno. Weave 2½″ (6.25 cm) plain weave. Weave 2½″ (6.25 cm) any leno variation bordered with weft float pattern in rust. Weave 4″ (10 cm) plain weave, one row of Spanish lace with rust, and 2″ plain weave with pale yellow. Weave 5″ (12.5 cm) Brooks bouquet, bordered with weft float pattern in rust. Reverse pattern from center of Brooks bouquet area. Weft float pattern—place heddle in down shed po-

sition. In the area behind the heddle, pick up only the slot warps in this sequence: 1 up, 2 down, all the way across. When pattern is desired, turn stick on edge, pass shuttle back and forth in this shed as many times as desired, catching the weft around the outside warp each time so it doesn't pull out.

FINISHING: Hemstitch each end, make decorative finish (page 104) with 3 rows of knots, and cut fringe 2½″ (6.25 cm) long. Even up the selvedges in the open weave areas and press with hot steam iron and damp cloth. □

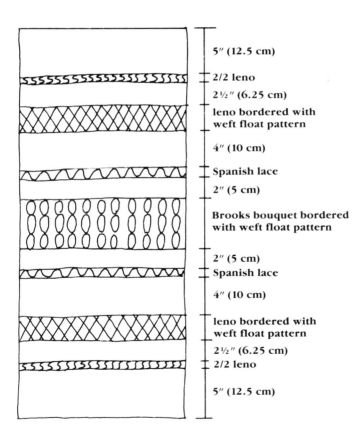

5″ (12.5 cm)

2/2 leno

2½″ (6.25 cm)

leno bordered with weft float pattern

4″ (10 cm)

Spanish lace

2″ (5 cm)

Brooks bouquet bordered with weft float pattern

2″ (5 cm)

Spanish lace

4″ (10 cm)

leno bordered with weft float pattern

2½″ (6.25 cm)

2/2 leno

5″ (12.5 cm)

Transparency Inlay

Designed by Betty Davenport　　　　　　　　　　　　*Woven by Dorothy Mucha*

FABRIC DESCRIPTION: Plain weave transparency with inlay.

FINISHED SIZE: 18″ (45 cm) square.

WARP: 10/2 line linen at 1350 yds/lb (2700 m/kg). This is from Frederick J. Fawcett: 195 yd (178 m) natural.

WEFT: 5/1 super slubby tow linen at 1500 yds/lb (3000 m/kg). This is from Frederick J. Fawcett: 100 yd (91 m) natural. **Inlay yarns**—small amounts of 7/2 wool at 1640 yd/lb (3280 m/kg) in two shades of red, 12/3 Oregon Worsted Nehalem at 2160 yd/lb (4325 m/kg) in dove gray, and purple sewing thread.

NOTIONS: 19″ (47.5 cm) long dowel.

E.P.I.: 10 (40/10 cm).

HEDDLE: 10-dent (40/10).

WIDTH IN HEDDLE: 18.5″ (46.5 cm).

TOTAL WARP ENDS: 186.

WARP LENGTH: 36″ (90 cm), which includes take-up, shrinkage, and 18″ (45 cm) loom waste.

WEFT ROWS PER INCH: 10 (40/10 cm).

WEAVING: Enlarge drawing on sheet of paper or nonwoven interfacing. Draw outlines with a wide marking pen. For the outside areas, use two strands of dove gray and two strands of sewing machine thread wound together in a butterfly. For the flower, use two strands of 7/2

wool wound together in a butterfly. Make a separate butterfly for each color area across the width of the warp.

FINISHING: Machine zigzag ends and turn a narrow hem at each end. Insert the dowel rod in the top hem for hanging. Press with a steam iron and a damp cloth. □

1 square = 1″ (2.5 cm)

USING A DRAWING

After you have enlarged the drawing on a sheet of sturdy paper or nonwoven interfacing, pin its lower edge to the first rows of your weaving. You will be able to see the drawing through the unwoven warp and to follow it as you weave. As the weaving advances, repin the drawing at the new fell whenever you need to. Unpin the section you have used so it will not roll onto the front beam with the finished weaving.

This simple inlay hanging will let in light while enhancing a view.

Surface Textures

The following techniques are worked within the plain weave fabric as weaving progresses. They make raised surface textures which you can use to vary your fabric.

Soumak

Soumak is like the outline stitch in embroidery, but it is worked as the cloth is woven. It can be added to either balanced or weft-faced plain weave. Some oriental rugs are constructed entirely in soumak technique.

The weft can be carried on a short shuttle or in a butterfly. Start on the left selvedge with a closed shed. Lay the weft yarn in a loop away from you, move over four warps and bring the shuttle back under two warps. Pull the weft snug. Repeat across the warp. Weave at least one

Soumak can be varied by the direction in which you work it and by the number of warps it travels across in each wrap. The diamond at the top was made with the diagonal technique explained on the next page.

row of plain weave after each soumak row, and remember to alternate the plain weave sheds.

The direction in which the soumak row slants depends on the direction in which it was worked. If you work from left to right each time, it will always slant the same way. If you alternate the edges from which you start, every two rows of soumak row will look like an embroidered chain stitch, instead of layers of outline stitch.

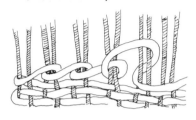

Pile can be long or short, dense or sparse, cut or uncut. Each knot can contain a single color, or several shades.

The number of warps over and under which the soumak weft travels can vary. Try going over two and back one, or over six and back two. You can work one or two rows of soumak as a border for another technique or use a different number of plain weave rows between soumak rows.

An interesting variation of soumak creates a diagonal line of texture. Using a contrasting pattern weft, work one soumak wrap within a row of plain weave. Weave several rows of plain weave, then work another soumak wrap a few warps over from where the first one was made. Weave several more plain weave rows, and so forth. You can control the angle of the diagonal line by the number of plain weave rows you use between soumak lines.

Pile techniques

Knots or loops can cover an entire piece, in the manner of the Scandinavian rya rugs, which were developed to imitate sheepskin rugs. They can also be used as accents, if a few rows of knots or loops are added to a wall hanging, pillow, or runner. Placed according to a plan, they can form free designs.

To create pile, draw loops of yarn to the surface of the weaving or tie short lengths of yarn around the warp ends. The loops can be cut or left as they are. Cut and uncut pile can be used in the same piece. Rows of plain weave between the loops or knots hold them in place.

Use a firmly twisted wool yarn for the pile. You can run a yarn of different texture or fiber along with the wool for variety and sparkle, but avoid yarns that ravel or shed loose fibers.

To work the pile from a **continuous length** of yarn, begin by winding three or four strands of yarn together in a butterfly. You'll work on a closed shed (heddle in neutral position) and make each knot around two warp ends. Push the butterfly down between the two warp ends, bring it up to the left of the lefthand warp, up to the right across both warps, down to the right of the righthand warp, and back up between the two warps next to the fell line.

Tighten the knot. The pile length is formed between the knots. Wrap the weft around your finger to form a loop; you will control the length

of the pile by the amount of yarn you use in the loop. Very small loops of uncut pile can be wrapped around a dowel rod, pencil, or knitting needle. Work the next knot around the next two warps and make another loop. Repeat across the warp.

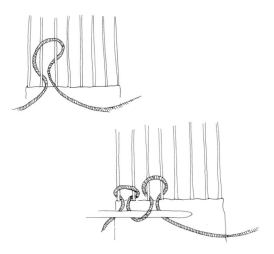

Knots made from a continuous piece of yarn.

Weave several rows of plain weave before you make another row of knots. If you want cut pile, snip each row of loops after it has been secured by some plain weave.

Making pile from **short lengths of yarn** allows you to use up miscellaneous bits of yarn, and you can change the colors that appear in each knot. Cut 3- to 4-inch (7.5 to 10 cm) lengths of yarn, in a single color or a variety of harmonizing colors. Use three or four strands together to tie each knot around two warps. Lay the strands over the two warps, then take the tails around and bring them up between the two warps and toward you. Tighten the knot until it's secure. Repeat this process across the warp. Weave several plain weave rows before you do another row of knots.

Knots made from short lengths of yarn.

The amount of plain weave between rows of knots depends on the length and thickness of your pile. Generally, the tips of the second row of pile should cover the knots of the previous row. Short pile with only a few rows of plain weave will stand up straight. Long pile with a lot of plain weave will lay flat.

Try making knots as a raised design against a plain weave background. The plain weave rows will have to be built up on each side of the raised design to fill in to the height of the knot, in the technique you used to combine plain weave with the open weave variations.

Tapestry

Tapestry offers more design freedom than any other weaving technique, but is also the slowest to weave. Each area of color is woven back and forth with its own weft. There is no background weft to bind the structure together, which makes the junctions between the wefts very important. A variety of techniques are used to join the areas where two colors meet. Traditionally, tapestry is weft-faced. Areas of tapestry can be combined with other weft-faced techniques. A small amount of tapestry can add a lot of impact to a wall hanging or runner of simple stripes or color-and-weave patterns. Tapestry techniques can also be used in weft-emphasis and balanced weave fabrics.

The tapestry techniques given here are very basic—just enough to give you a taste of what tapestry has to offer. More advanced techniques can be explored with the help of one of the many books devoted to this type of weaving.

At first it is best to work with geometric shapes or very simple drawings. Many striking designs can be made by repeating one shape, like a triangle or a square.

The sett and weaving methods are the same as for weft-faced plain weave. The weft yarn is usually wool, which is easy to handle and packs in firmly. Wind the weft yarns into butterflies, but don't make them too large or you'll have a hard time maneuvering them around the warp ends.

There are two basic methods of building up the design. Each row can consist of one pick of each weft color, laid in its area in sequence across the width of the warp, keeping the fell line level. This method is faster for geometric

shapes and has the advantage that the heddle can be used to beat the wefts into place. Freeform shapes are easier to weave if each color area is built up separately. Each different color weaves back and forth in its own area; a tapestry beater or table fork will be needed for beating the weft into place, since some areas will build up more quickly than others and the fell line will be uneven.

There are also two ways to move the butterflies. They can all travel in the same direction in a given shed—for example, from right to left. Or they can *meet-and-separate,* so each butterfly moves in the direction opposite to that of its two neighbors. For your introduction to tapestry, I will concentrate here on meet-and-separate.

You can understand the expression *meet-and-separate* by beginning to work with only two butterflies. One begins at the *right* selvedge, travels to the left through the shed, and is pulled up to the surface of the weaving between two warp ends at the point where you want the second color to begin appearing. The second butterfly begins at the *left* selvedge, travels to the right through the shed, and comes up between the same two warp ends. With the two butterflies sitting on top of the weaving, you change sheds. Tuck in the beginning tails of yarn. The first butterfly goes back down between warp ends into the new shed and takes a return trip to the right selvedge. The second butterfly enters the new shed and revisits the left selvedge. They meet in the middle, and separate to go back to their original positions.

It is helpful to practice tapestry techniques first on a sampler where you will have only two colors. Become comfortable with each technique before you move to the next. Once you're familiar with the basics, try weaving with three or four color areas and combining several techniques. Each technique will suggest the types of designs for which it is most effective.

In tapestry you will find that horizontal and diagonal lines are much easier to weave than are vertical lines, which leave long slits unless the adjoining wefts are interlocked as you weave. It's also very challenging to keep the warps from pulling apart where vertical shapes meet. If you find you have planned a tapestry with a lot of vertical lines, turn the design sideways and weave it that way: your vertical joins will become horizontal lines and will be simple to weave.

Vertical slit

A vertical color change is made by always turning the wefts around the same warp ends. This will leave a slit that can be stitched up later by hand, or the slit can be part of your design. Vertical shapes must be at least two warp threads wide.

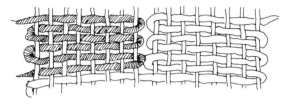

Vertical joins

There are several ways to join the edges of a vertical slit during the weaving process. Each has a characteristic appearance. The easiest, and the one to which I'll limit myself here, is the *dovetail,* in which the two colors at the join turn around the same warp. Since both wefts reverse directions on the same warp, there will be twice as many wefts on that warp as there are picks in the surrounding area. This builds up thickness in the area of the join and so is best for short distances. The join will be neatest if you consistently move the same weft *first* each time. This join also works well in weft-emphasis or balanced weave fabrics.

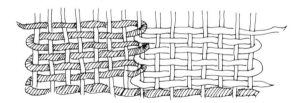

Diagonals

To make a diagonal edge between colors, two butterflies meet and separate as described. On the next shed, bring the first butterfly out in the same position. The second butterfly meets it. Change sheds. Each of the butterflies will turn to go back to its selvedge *one warp to the left* of where it turned on the last pick. Weave each butterfly back to its selvedge. On each subsequent row, move both butterflies one warp end to the left.

When you understand this movement, reverse directions and make the angle move to the right, one warp at a time.

To get a *steeper angle,* make two turns around the same warp before moving over. An even

steeper angle can be achieved if you make three turns around each warp before moving to the next.

A *shallower angle* is produced by moving over more warp ends with each change.

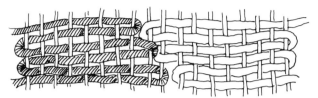

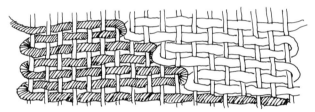

The basic diagonal: one warp at a time.

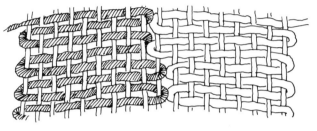

The steeper diagonal.

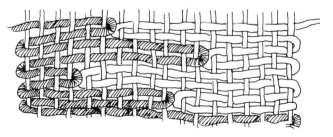

The shallower diagonal.

Hatching

Hatching is a way of blending two color areas. The hatched area can follow a definite outline or it can be irregular. Start two butterflies, one from each selvedge, and bring them out at the right-hand end of the area to be hatched. Change sheds and move the butterflies back to their edges. In the next shed, the butterflies again move toward each other but will meet at the *lefthand* edge of the area to be hatched. The spot where the butterflies meet will alternate between the righthand and lefthand edges of the area.

Hatching can be used to form regular shapes or to make irregular, shaded areas. Play with it!

WARP: 8/4 linen rug warp at 260 yd/lb (520 m/kg): 42 yd (39 m).

WEFT: Singles wool at 784 yd/lb (1570 m/kg). This is Top of the Lamb from Brown Sheep Company, available in 196 yd (178 m)/4 oz skeins: 1 skein each of Framboise #311 and Seaglass #370. 85% wool/15% mohair singles at 784 yd/lb (1570 m/kg). This is Lamb's Pride, size #1, from Brown Sheep Company, available in 196 yd (178 m)/4 oz skeins: 1 skein Boysenberry #55. *This is the same yarn used for the first project. If you wove the project with the measurements we suggested, you will have enough yarn left to make this tapestry purse.*

E.P.I.: 5 (20/10 cm).

HEDDLE: 10-dent (40/10). Thread for half-density (see p. 99).

WIDTH IN HEDDLE: 8″ (20 cm).

TOTAL WARP ENDS: 40.

WARP LENGTH: 1 yd (90 cm), which includes 18″ (45 cm) loom waste.

WEAVING: Follow the diagram, using the tapestry techniques described in this chapter where they are indicated.

Note 1: The diagonal on the diagram will not necessarily match the diagonal which you weave; this isn't a problem. Let the angle weave at its own diagonal rate for ¾″ (1.8 cm), then reverse for ¾″ (1.8 cm) and you should be back at the center.

Note 2: When it's time to do the hatched diamond, let the diagonal establish its own angle again. If the diagonal seems too shallow, work 2 rows on each side before moving over a warp end.

When you reach the last ½″ (1.25 cm), leave the outside 6 warps on each side unwoven for ¼″ (.75 cm), following the diagram, and then leave the outside 12 warps on each side unwoven for ¼″ (.75 cm) while you finish the center section as shown.

ASSEMBLY: Tie warps together in pairs with overhand knots and then weave in the ends (see p. 101). Fold purse up at arrows marked A and sew side seam neatly. Fold purse down at arrows marked B. Mark position for button under buttonhole. Make and attach button.

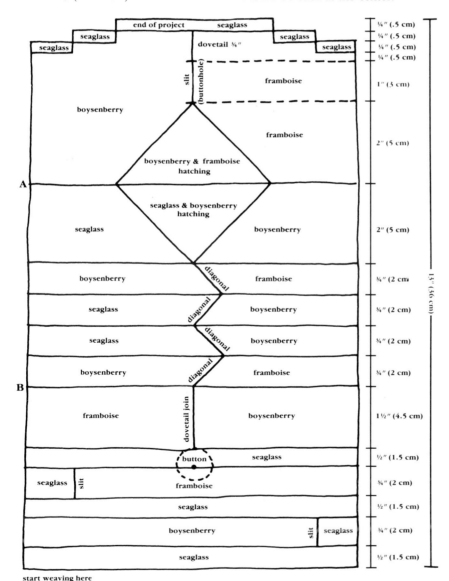

Button for the Purse

Wrap Seaglass around a pencil 20 times, letting the turns pile up on each other to make a ball. Using the same strand, measure 1 yard (90 cm) of Seaglass, cut the yarn, and thread the end in a blunt needle. Carefully slide the ball of yarn off the pencil, holding the hole between thumb and forefinger. With the blunt needle, go through the hole. Choose one or two strands at the equator of the ball and take a stitch under them. Repeat, alternately wrapping through the hole and taking a stitch at the equator until the ball is completely covered. Use the yarn tail to sew the button to the purse. ☐

With the leftover yarns from the first project, you can make this charming tapestry bag. It includes all the tapestry techniques explained in the text and an ingenious button.

On Your Own

When you are learning to weave, the decisions involved in planning a project on your own can seem overwhelming. As you do your own planning, you'll find that if you move one step at a time and ask yourself the right questions, you'll get all the information you need to produce successful finished weavings.

Planning a Project

If you have trouble getting started, using the "recipes" published in weaving magazines or booklets may help. Often you will find that you want to customize the instructions by changing the colors or types of yarn specified. It's not important whether you start from scratch or use a published project plan. What counts is that you start.

Whether you find a project in one of the printed sources or plan from scratch, evaluate your selection and guide your planning with a similar set of questions.

What size should it be?
—Is this scarf long enough to go around your neck and hang as long as you want?
—Is this placemat large enough to accommodate a place setting and napkin and leave a border showing? Use a tape measure to determine these measurements.

What kind of yarn?
—Is this scarf soft against your skin? Is the scarf warm (wool or mohair) or a fashion accent (silk or rayon might be nice)?
—Is this placemat machine washable? If you're willing to iron, consider linen.

What color?
—Is your scarf to match your winter coat, or your eyes, or a special suit?
—Are your mats to use with a particular set of dishes? Or to match the wallpaper? Or to camouflage food spots?

You might simply fall in love with a particular yarn. In this case, it's necessary to work in reverse and decide on a project that is appropriate for the yarn.

Once you choose your yarn and your project, you will need to ask:
—How much yarn will it take?
A project record sheet, like the one found under "Calculating amounts of yarn" on page 93, will take you step by step through the simple math used to figure the number of yards you need. Begin a worksheet for your project at this point, and start filling in the blanks with the figures you know now.

From each project you will gain invaluable experience that will make the next project easier. Another set of questions covers evaluation:
—What would you do differently next time?
—Is the size appropriate to your intentions? Should the next project of the same type be longer? Wider?
—Did the yarns work well?
—Do you like the colors?

Before you know it, you will have gained enough experience that designing from scratch will be a breeze.

Project Ideas

Your rigid heddle loom can produce an unlimited variety of fabrics for an equally large number of purposes. You can find or adapt projects which use narrow fabrics or you can sew panels together. Looms as narrow as 20 inches (50 cm), or even 14 inches (35 cm), can produce large weavings if you join panels to obtain wider pieces of cloth. The following list of ideas and guidelines will help expand your horizons.

Pillows. Unless pillows are to be purely decorative, they need to be able to withstand some wear. Fabrics can be of any type, in any yarn that is pleasant to touch. Exciting designs can be developed from the color-and-weave patterns or from the hand-controlled techniques.

Pillow sizes can vary. A good general size for a sofa accent pillow is in the range of 14 to 18 inches (35 to 45 cm), but you may want to make floor cushions or pincushions. You can weave the outer fabric to fit a ready-made pillow form or you can construct your own pillow casing and stuff it.

If your pillow fabric is weft-faced, you may find that machine-stitched seams become very bulky when the seam allowance is turned to the inside. If you want to minimize bulk, knot the warps of the two ends together to close one edge, in the method described for the finishing of the first project, and close the remaining sides by needleweaving or whipstitching the selvedges together.

Scarves and stoles. The fabrics for scarves and stoles should be soft, drapable, and pleasant to feel against the skin. Soft wools and mohairs are always good choices, and you may want to consider some of the luxury fibers, like silk, alpaca, or cashmere, or some of the textured novelty yarns that are popular for knitting. Scarves in particular require relatively small amounts of yarn and an investment in special, soft yarns can be worthwhile.

To achieve softness and good draping qualities, use a balanced weave with a medium to open sett but beat lightly. There are no standard sizes for scarves and stoles. Measure an existing piece which you like, or drape muslin around yourself and measure it when it falls to the length you want.

Placemats and runners. Placemats that are easy to wash and require no ironing are likely to be used and enjoyed every day. Yarns of cotton or cotton-linen blends are quite carefree; linen needs ironing. Textured yarns camouflage wrinkles.

Any of the techniques in this book can be used for mats or runners, and the open weaves and inlays make excellent borders or designs. A good size for placemats is approximately 12 by 18 inches (30 × 45 cm), finished. A generous size for matching napkins is 16 or 20 inches (40 cm, 50 cm) square. Fringe is a popular finish, but if

Tapestry is often used on weft-faced fabrics, but can also be effective on a balanced weave. Note how the colors of the warp stripes are modified by the weft colors.

you don't like the look of frayed fringe, plan to hand wash the mats or to turn up a hem.

Table runners used primarily for decoration are not subjected to the wear that placemats must tolerate. A wider range of fibers is appropriate. You could make a small mat to go with a table arrangement or a long scarf to drape over a dresser. The size will be determined by where you plan to use the runner.

Garments. Many garment styles can be made from narrow fabrics if you join several panels. Ethnic garments are usually constructed from rectangular pieces obtained from narrow fabric widths. Ethnic garments like caftans, ponchos, and smocks offer wonderful inspiration for garments designed on this basis; the resulting clothing can be contemporary-looking or can retain a sense of its roots.

Garment fabrics need to have a nice drapable hand, like that produced by a balanced weave. All natural fiber yarns are appropriate, except for coarse wools, which can be scratchy.

Tabards fit all sorts of people and occasions. This neatly fitted version uses three closely related colors in one of the simplest color-and-weave effects.

FABRIC DESCRIPTION: Plain weave.

SIZE: Can be adjusted to fit all sizes (see "Assembly" below). Length from shoulder to hem is 21″ (52.5 cm) and width is 20″ (50 cm).

WARP: Two-ply wool at 1650 yd/lb (3300 m/kg). We've used Novi-wool from Novitex, one spool each of Natural #102 and Nutria #40.

WEFT: Three-ply alpaca at 1850 yd/lb (3700 m/kg). We've used Indieceta from Plymouth Yarns, four 50-gram balls of white. The wool that's used in the warp also is suitable for weft, but will shrink up to 20% in width, and you'll have to plan accordingly (adjust width in heddle to about 23″/57.5 cm). One spool of Novi-wool will provide enough weft.

E.P.I.: 8 (32/10 cm).

HEDDLE: 8 (32/10).

WIDTH IN HEDDLE: 20″ (50 cm).

TOTAL WARP ENDS: 160.

WARP LENGTH: 2 yd (1.8 m), which includes take-up, shrinkage, and 18″ (45 cm) loom waste.

WARP COLOR ORDER:

		7 ×	
Natural		1	104
Nutria	40	1	

WEFT ROWS PER INCH: 9-10 (36-40/10 cm).

WEAVING: Wind shuttle with two strands of alpaca; the weft is used double. Weave plain weave to the end of the warp. (If you are using the wool as weft, do not double it.)

FINISHING: Secure ends with two overlapping rows of machine zigzag. The alpaca is very slick; one row of stitching along tends to pull out. Hand wash fabric using very warm water and a mild detergent. Rinse well, roll in a towel to extract water, and lay flat to dry. Steam press fabric while still slightly damp.

ASSEMBLY: Mark shoulder line and neck opening as shown. Baste-stitch shoulder line. Notice that the front is 1″ (2.5 cm) longer than the back to allow for a bust dart. Sew two rows of overlapping zigzag along the cutting lines. Trim out the neck opening. Finish the neckline with blanket stitch in alpaca worked over eight strands of natural wool.

At each shoulder line, fold the selvedge under 1½″ (3.75 cm). Taper the fold to nothing at the waist line. Stitch in place by hand. Now try on the tabard to decide how to close the sides. Small sizes can overlap the selvedges and secure the waist with Velcro fasteners. Medium sizes can make twisted or braided yarn ties, as described in this chapter. Large sizes can weave separate underarm panels.

While you are trying the tabard on for size, mark the bust points with pins and use these to position shallow darts. Mark the length and turn up a hem. □

Blanket stitch for neckline.

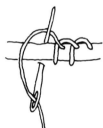

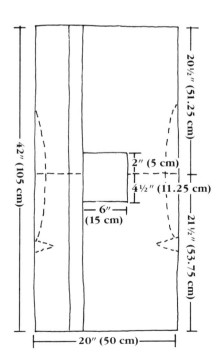

Good Design: A Handful of Tools

Everyone has the ability to create an original design. For some that ability is intuitive; if you feel comfortable making your own designs and choosing colors, read no further in this section. For others, it is a matter of hard work, trial and error, and self-training. Those of you who have just come to weaving without a background of design basics and who would like some tangible guidelines will find some here. Even beginning weaving efforts can be well designed, and you will continue to enjoy weaving when you are pleased with your results. I've brought together here the information I wish I'd known when I started to weave.

Learning about design is a lot like learning to juggle. Tossing one ball and catching it is relatively easy. Handling two balls takes a little more coordination and concentration, but once you've mastered the idea you can move to juggling three balls, and so on.

You can approach the principles of good design step by step through the elements of proportion and color. Start with an original design idea or color combination. If it doesn't look right, apply the guidelines presented here. Perhaps a slight adjustment will help make your basic design dynamic. If you want to, you can work through the specific exercises a few times. You'll find you will develop an instinctive feel for good proportion.

A good design or color combination will
1. please you.
2. suit its purpose.
3. have a unifying feature.
4. have variety and interest.

Proportion

Rectangles. Since most weavings are rectangular by nature, the first two factors to think about are (1) the proportion of length to width and (2) the division of space within it. A pleasing shape should be decisive. It should be a definite square or a definite rectangle. A shape that is not-quite-either will be disturbing to look at. A weaving should, of course, fit the space for which it is intended.

The world would be pretty dull if every rectangular item fit only one proportion. Books, typing paper, TVs, and computer monitors are all familiar rectangular shapes with proportions of about 1:1.3.

Many rectangles have a proportion (ratio) of 1:1.5, the length being 1.5 times the width. Another way to express the same ratio in whole numbers is 2:3, or two units in width to 3 units in length.

THE GOLDEN RECTANGLE

The rectangle which is often described as having the most pleasing proportions is called the Golden Rectangle, and its length is 1.618 times its width. The Greeks used this relationship in their art and architecture. If you know the width of a piece and want to find out how long to weave a Golden Rectangle, multiply the width by 1.6. If you know the length and want to know how wide to weave a Golden Rectangle, divide the length by 1.6.

You can construct a Golden Rectangle with no tools other than a piece of graph paper. Although it is easier to use a calculator and multiply the ratio, it is helpful to understand the geometry of the relationship. Then you can make a quick calculation at the loom, using a measuring tape, string, or whatever is handy.

Cut a narrow strip from one side of the paper to use as a measure. Draw a square shape on the larger piece of graph paper; a 10-by-10 section will simplify calculations. Mark the center of the square's lower edge. Place the strip of graph paper in a diagonal line from this center point to the upper righthand corner of the square and mark this length on the strip. Swivel the measuring strip down to the base line to extend the base of the square into a rectangle. You'll see that the size of the new rectangle is 10 by 16 units: a ratio of 1:1.6.

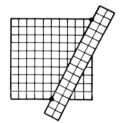

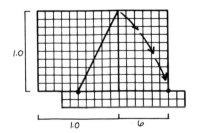

The Golden Rectangle is developed from the diagonal of *half* a square, but other pleasing rectangles can be developed from the diagonal of the full square. Draw another 10-by-10 square and measure its diagonal with your paper strip. Swivel the measure down again to extend the baseline of the square into that of a different rectangle. The size of this figure (#2) will be 10 by 14 units, or 1:1.4. Now draw a diagonal through this rectangle, swivel it down to extend the base further into a rectangle (#3) with a ratio of 1:1.7. Repeat; the rectangle (#4) will have a ratio of 1:2. Repeat once again; the final rectangle (#5) will have a ratio of 1:2.2.

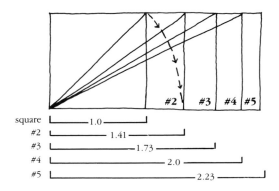

A series of interesting rectangles can be developed from the diagonal of a full square.

Now that you've developed these rectangles and know their ratios, you can use a calculator to apply the ratios to any project.

Dividing space into smaller areas. We can systematically divide the rectangle into units which will relate to the size of the whole. For a weaving this will help us place a pattern, or stripes, or the center of interest.

An interesting thing about the series of rectangles you just developed from the square is that each can be divided into smaller units which all have the same proportions as the whole. Rectangle #2 divided into two smaller rectangles, #3 into three, and so forth. The size of this smaller area can be determined by dividing the short side of the rectangle by the ratio. For instance, divide the short side of rectangle #3 (10 units) by 1.7. The result is 5.9. The three smaller rectangles which can be fitted into the large rectangle will be just under 6 units wide and will have the same width to length ratio as the original rectangle.

These rectangles, with their proportionally related divisions, have a rhythm and life to them. Use these ratios when you plan a project in which you want the design to appear in equal-sized sections.

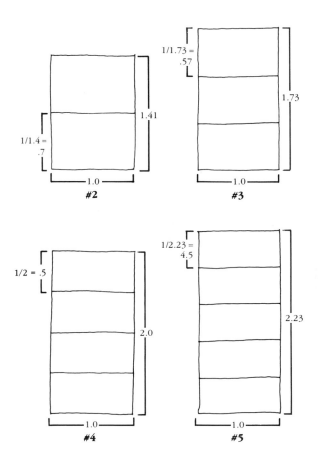

Any rectangle can be divided into two unequal but related areas if you mark off a shape at one end that has the same proportions as the whole. First find the ratio of length to width (divide the length by the width). Divide the rectangle's width by that ratio to find the distance from the edge at which you will draw a vertical line. The smaller space will have the same proportions as the large space.

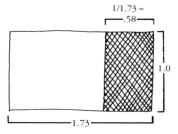

Same proportion

You can get another pleasing division if you multiply the length by .6 and draw a line at that point. Or multiply the width by .6 and draw a horizontal line at that point. Multiplying by .6 produces another approximation of the 1:1.5 relationship discussed earlier. If you use both vertical and horizontal divisions, the rectangle will contain four parts, two of which will have the same proportions as the whole. These guidelines can be used for the general placement of a curved line or other shape, and the point where the lines intersect can locate the focal point for a design.

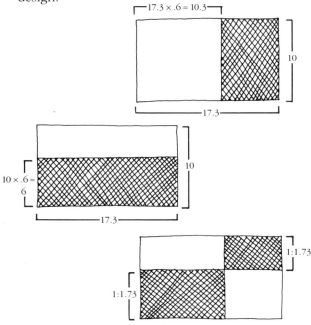

You can make a small rectangle which bears the same proportions as its larger host and center it within the large rectangle. This rectangle with a border will have a liveliness you can't get by measuring in from each edge by an equal amount and drawing a rectangle.

Your guides for the inner rectangle will be diagonal lines drawn from corner to corner on the larger shape. Draw the inner rectangle with its corners touching the diagonal lines. It can be any size.

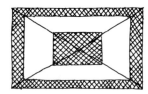

Smaller area is in proportion

You can make small rectangles this way, and use several of them on the larger rectangle. You can determine their placement by constructing one of the frames. You can connect a series of large and small rectangles with the same proportions to develop designs for borders, a long runner, or a scarf.

Above, *several rectangles of the same proportions are set into a large rectangle, making a pleasing design.* Left, *a series of large and small rectangles of the same proportions are connected to make a long project.*

As you can see, there are many pleasing rectangles and an infinite number of ways to divide the space into related areas. Use these guidelines to help yourself develop original ideas. You will find they are quite flexible as you discover new ways of applying them. Remember, though, that always following the rules can lead to predictability and boredom. Once you have a principle firmly in mind, experiment with it to bring liveliness and excitement to your work.

Lines: the Fibonacci series. There are many possible proportion sequences for designing a pattern of stripes. One way to design interesting lines or stripes is by using a progressive series of numbers known as the *Fibonacci* or *summation series*. Fibonacci, a thirteenth-century mathematician, arrived at this number series as the solution to a problem he posed about the number of rabbits that could be propagated from one pair in one year. The series goes: 1, 1, 2, 3, 5, 8, 13, 21, 34, and so forth. Each number in the series is the sum of the two previous numbers. The relationship between each pair of numbers is, amazingly enough, approximately 1:1.618, which you'll remember from the Golden Rectangle. It has also been found to relate to the growth patterns found in nature. Using the ratios in the Fibonacci series gives a sense of movement and rhythm to the stripes and patterns in our weaving designs.

However, just as there are rectangles other than the Golden Rectangle, there are number series other than Fibonacci's. For example, if each number in a series increases by one unit from the previous number, the series becomes 1, 2, 3, 4, 5. If it increases by three units, the series is 1, 4, 7, 10. Or each number can increase over the preceding number by a fixed percentage.

Use any method of creating a number series that looks interesting. The important point is that there is some kind of relationship between the numbers. By working with the Fibonacci series a few times, however, you will develop a feel for rhythmic intervals and be able to develop stripes more instinctively.

USING THE FIBONACCI SERIES

You can make use of the ratios of the Fibonacci series, or any other number series, in a lot of different ways. Here are some ideas. Choose one and play with it, then come back for more.

1. Each number in the series can represent the width of a stripe. Use that number of threads, centimeters, inches, or any size of unit.
2. A sequence of numbers from the series can be repeated as much as you like (2, 3, 5, 2, 3, 5, and so forth).
3. A sequence can be used and then reversed (1, 3, 5, 3, 1).
4. The numbers can be taken out of sequence (3, 8, 1, 5).
5. One of the numbers in a series can be repeated (1, 1, 1, 5, 1, 1, 1).
6. The location for single stripes in borders can be located through the number series (measure in inches, centimeters, threads, or what-have-you).
7. If you set up a repeat of stripe widths based on the series (1, 2, 5, and repeat) and use a number of colors which is one more or less than the number of stripes in a repeat (in this case, either two or four colors), the colors will rotate to different widths of stripes across your fabric.
8. The spaces between units (like the placement of a textured yarn, or an inch of pattern) can be determined according to the series, in one of its varying applications, or the spaces between units can be equal and the sizes of the units (stripes or pattern) can be determined through the series.
9. You can use the series to gradually blend from one color to another (for example, thread or weave 1 dark, 3 light, 2 dark, 2 light, 3 dark, 1 light).

RATIO is the relationship of one part to another.

To find the RATIO OF A RECTANGLE, divide its length by its width.

If the proposed design is to have EQUAL-SIZED DIVISIONS, apply the ratio for the rectangle, which will divide it into units of the same proportions.

Use these divisions as GUIDELINES, not straitjackets. You can place curves or areas of emphasis along them, as well as straight lines.

When you want to PLAN A DESIGN ON GRAPH PAPER, use one square of the paper to represent one inch or centimeter of your design.

If your ORIGINAL DESIGN NEEDS HELP, systematically section your rectangle according to the guidelines and see if the results indicate a minor change which could make an enormous difference.

Cotton carpet warp is inexpensive, readily available, and comes in a variety of colors. This vest makes use of it, and the idea of grouping yarns in warp and weft, for a practical garment which can go almost anywhere. In construction, the fabric is turned so the warp runs horizontally; the fabric width determines the length of the vest. If you want a longer vest, you can weave wider fabric.

82

Designed by Betty Davenport

FABRIC DESCRIPTION: Plain weave with grouped warps and wefts.

SIZE: Women's large; circumference at chest 42" (105 cm), length at center back 17½" (43.75 cm).

WARP & WEFT: 8/4 cotton carpet warp at 1600 yd/lb (3200 m/kg): 1345 yd (1224 m) red.

NOTIONS: Tapestry needle, sewing needle, matching thread, 5 buttons, size 8 crochet hook.

E.P.I.: Overall average of 16 ends per inch (64/10 cm), with 12 ends per inch (48/10 cm) in plain weave areas.

HEDDLE: 12-dent (48/10).

WIDTH IN HEDDLE: 20" (50 cm).

TOTAL WARP ENDS: 336.

WARP LENGTH: 2 yds (188 cm), which includes shrinkage, take-up, and 18" (45 cm) loom waste.

DRAFT:

WEFT ROWS PER INCH: 12 (48/10 cm) in plain weave areas, 16 (64/10 cm) overall.

WEAVING: Weave 24 rows plain weave laying the weft in at a generous angle. Then weave 5 rows in the same shed to make a row of grouped wefts; lay the weft at a shallower angle than previously. Be sure to catch the weft around the outside warp and beat it in place each time. Try to keep the 5 wefts lying parallel to each other in the shed. Repeat this sequence to the end of the warp.

FINISHING: Zigzag warp ends. Machine wash in cool water and dry in dryer. Iron while still slightly damp.

ASSEMBLY: For large size, measure 47" (117.5 cm). Zigzag raw edges.

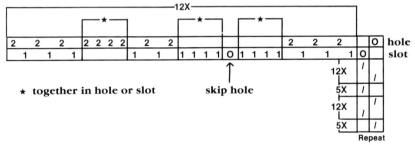

★ **together in hole or slot**   **skip hole**

THREADING: Thread the loops from the warp cross through the slots in this order: 1 loop each in 3 slots, 2 loops together in the next 4 slots, 1 loop each in 3 slots, repeat. Start the first loop 10" (25 cm) to the right of center in your heddle. The warp yarns are now properly spaced for threading the heddle once the warp is wound. After you've wound on, thread the heddle in this order:

6 threads single in each slot and hole,
4 threads together in a slot, skip a hole,
4 threads together in a slot,
4 threads single in each hole and slot,
4 threads together in a hole,
6 threads single in each slot and hole,
repeat.

Fold back 1½" (3.75 cm) on each end for front facing. Lay fabric flat and fold the ends to the center, overlapping them 1" (2.5 cm) for the front closure (illustration 1). To make armholes, mark side folds and sew two lines of zigzag stitching 11" (27.5 cm) down from top, and cut between the two lines of stitching. (Note: always double stitch, overlapping the rows slightly.) Mark front neckline and stitch 1½" (3.75 cm) out from it to allow for the facing. Trim away excess (illustration 2).

For shoulder seams, turn piece inside out. Start stitching at the selvedge edge 4½" (11.25 cm) in from the armhole edge. Stitch on the diagonal toward a point 1" (2.5 cm) down from the selvedge on the armhole edge. End stitching 1" (2.5 cm) from armhole edge so that when the armhole facing is folded back, the excess shoulder seam fabric can also be folded back, opened flat, and tacked down on top of it. (You should have a flat triangular shoulder seam when done.) Turn back center front and neckline facings and hand stitch in place. I use the catch stitch, which helps the facing lie smoothly without showing on the front. To finish armhole, turn back and hand stitch a 1" (2.5 cm) facing around the armhole, tapering to a point at the bottom. With a tapestry needle and some warp thread, overcast the raw edges at the bottom of the armhole to reinforce it.

You will notice an empty notch in the neckline at the shoulder seam (illustration 3). From the scraps, cut a triangular piece large enough to turn back a 1" (2.5 cm) hem at the neck edge. Zigzag edges well. Fit triangular piece under the opening and hand stitch in place. Catch stitch the edges down. This little gusset allows 1" (2.5 cm) extra in length to the vest. To shape back neckline, fold over ½" (1.25 cm) at center and taper to nothing at the shoulderline. Hand stitch down. Measure 8 strands of cotton warp the length of the bottom edge of the vest. Overcast this bundle right on the selvedge edge using a tapestry needle and a length of warp yarn. Hide the ends of the bundles in the front facings. Space the stitches so they match the woven area. Crochet button loops on the right side. Sew on the buttons. □

Illustration 1.

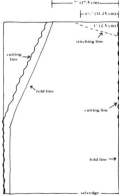

Illustration 2.

Illustration 3.

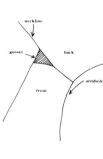

heddle loom, you will need to be particularly careful that the slot thread layer does not end up looser than the hole thread layer. If you forget to put the heddle in the up shed position before you tie the warp onto the front beam, you'll have trouble. It may be wisest to lash the warp onto the front beam. Tension oddities seem to be easier to tame that way.

Linen comes from the long fibers in the stem of the flax plant. Yarns made from these fibers are called *line;* they have a nice sheen and are very strong and smooth. The processing of flax also produces short, broken fibers which are called *tow;* yarns spun from them have a fuzzy texture and will shed in washing. A singles tow yarn can be very difficult to use in a warp on a rigid heddle loom, because the friction of the heddle's movement can fray it until it breaks.

Rayon is made from chemically processed cellulose. Rayon drapes well but can be limp if it is woven loosely. Yarns made from rayon can be very shiny or matte and are often textured novelties. Rayon is delicate and requires gentle laundering, more like that of wool than of cotton or linen.

Acrylic is a synthetic fiber made to imitate wool in loftiness and warmth. Acrylic yarns are less expensive than wool and a real boon to those with wool allergies. The fiber is very strong and machine washable, but tends to pill easily. Acrylic knitting worsted is difficult to handle as a weaving yarn, especially for a beginner, because it is so spongy and stretchy. If you use an acrylic yarn for a project, keep your tension as loose as possible and beat lightly.

Blends are yarns made of two or more fibers; they combine the characteristics of the fibers included. A wool and silk blend produces a yarn with the luster of silk and loftiness of wool. A cotton and linen blend has linen's body and cotton's softness and drape. Another way to combine fiber qualities is to ply strands of different fibers together. Many novelty yarns designed for knitting are made in this way and will work well for weaving projects.

Choosing a warp yarn

The safest yarns to use as warp are smooth and have two or more plies. Many other types of yarns can also be used as warp, but need to be tested before you commit yourself to using them in a big project.

To test a yarn to find out if it is suitable for use in a warp, first hold three or four strands between your hands and pull firmly, to simulate the loom's tension. Give the yarns a snap; this will help you forecast how they will hold up under the stress of sudden tension changes, as when you change sheds. Then snap a single strand between your hands to see if it's likely to break if you snag it with your shuttle. If the yarn is textured, run your fingers back and forth over a section of it to see if any of the textural elements move or bunch up. If they do, the same will happen when the heddle rubs back and forth, and you'll find yourself with many frayed or broken ends. Then thread several strands through the holes and slots of the heddle. Pull them back and forth a few times to see if the yarn runs through without catching or shredding. Often a textured yarn that catches in the holes can still be used safely for slot threads. Keep in mind that the more closely you set the textured yarns the more friction they will experience in the heddle.

Some singles yarns will be strong enough for use as warp, especially if they have been spun from long fibers and have been firmly twisted. However, singles yarns that are fuzzy or have been spun from short fibers will tend to shred and break. If you can rough up the fibers in a singles yarn with your fingernails it will also fray in the heddle. If you want to use these yarns in a warp, wait until you are feeling very patient or are looking for a challenge.

Handspun two-ply yarns are satisfactory for use as warp yarns with the rigid heddle as long as they have no big bumps that will catch in the holes. A handspun singles made from a long-staple fiber will be strong enough if it has been smoothly spun with sufficient twist.

Sampling

Weaving a small sample before you start a project eliminates guesswork and gives you a chance to see how the yarns and colors will interact before you commit a lot of yarn and time to the larger piece. Sampling is one of the fastest ways to gain experience. The investment in yarn and time is well spent. The hardest part is getting in the habit of doing it!

If the sampling process is quick and easy, you will be more likely to take advantage of it. Here's a method I've devised that lets me measure and design a sample warp right on the rigid heddle loom. This technique gives a sample big enough to be useful, lets you discover how well the yarns you have in mind will work in the heddle and at the sett you've chosen, and doesn't waste yarn.

Once your loom is ready, it will take you less than forty-five minutes to prepare and complete your sample. Knowing ahead of time that your idea will work successfully will make the weaving process more pleasant and ensure your satisfaction with the finished product.

If your loom has plastic teeth on the beams, you will warp around them. If your loom does not have teeth, spend a few moments to make a device which serves the same purpose from a piece of screen door lath and a handful of small brads. It will be invaluable every time you want to sample. Cut a 10-inch length of lath. Mark it at 1-inch (2.5 cm) intervals. Nail the brads into the lath, using five brads equally spaced in every inch (one on each mark and four between each set of marks). Loop the lath through the extension cords, then tape it securely onto the back beam or cross brace while you measure the warp.

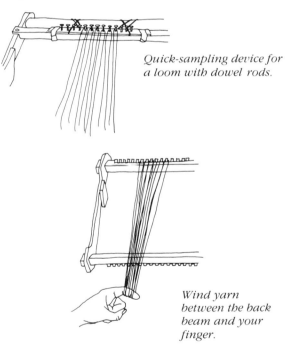

Quick-sampling device for a loom with dowel rods.

Wind yarn between the back beam and your finger.

I generally make the warp for my samples between 4 and 8 inches (10 and 20 cm) wide and between 18 and 24 inches (45 and 60 cm) long. The length depends on how many weft variations I want to try and on how much yarn I can spare for the sample. Do plan to weave at least 4 inches (10 cm) of each weft variation. You could often place several options side by side in the warp (for instance, several stripe patterns can be incorporated in a single sample warp). However,

I prefer to make a series of samples, since the first will suggest changes to make for the second, and so forth.

Set aside the heddle, and wind the warp yarn back and forth between the teeth or brads at the back beam and your fingers. As you wind, each turn will tend to become slightly shorter than the last. Hold your finger at an angle toward you to counteract this tendency; then your warp ends will be even in length.

As you wind the yarn back and forth, you can easily change colors to make stripes or even go back to delete colors or make other changes. Since the warp is spread out in front of you, these decisions are easy to make.

When you are happy with the warp arrangement, cut the end loops at your finger. I generally wind the back beam around one turn, or until the cut ends are even with the front beam. This provides enough friction so the warps won't slip and become uneven as they are threaded through the heddle. If they shift, it will take a lot of time to even them up again.

Place the heddle in the heddle holder or clamp it so it stays steady. Pull the warp ends through the holes and slots of the heddle with a crochet hook. If the bottom of the heddle is marked, it will be easy to line up the warp from back to front. Tie 1-inch (2.5 cm) groups of warps in overhand knots and lash the knots to the front beam with a piece of string (see page 52). Even up the tension of each group. Weave a few rows with scrap yarn to spread the warp evenly.

Quick samples will give you a good idea of how the colors in the warp and weft will blend, how the proportions and colors balance in stripes and plaids, and how color-and-weave patterns will look. It is more difficult to determine the hand and drape of a fabric from a sample. In order to get an idea of these factors, you will need a sample at least 8 inches (20 cm) wide. If the warp for your actual project will be wider than your sample, you will need to compensate for the fact that weft tends to pack in more tightly on a narrow warp than it does on a wide one. To use your sample accurately, use a light touch on the beater and pay special attention to the number of picks you get per inch. If you find that you have to beat very hard on the 8-inch (20 cm) sample to get a balanced fabric, it will be impossible to achieve the same number of picks per inch on a 20-inch-wide (50 cm) warp.

Calculating amounts of yarn

Once you have decided on a project, chosen the yarn, and determined the sett, the next step is to figure out how much yarn to buy. A record sheet like the one pictured here makes it easy to get this information. Feel free to make copies of this record sheet for your own use. You just start filling in spaces!

First, make a layout of your proposed project. You can do this on the back of the record sheet. Start with the size of the finished piece. As an example, we'll figure out how much yarn is needed for a scarf that will be 8 by 54 inches (20 × 135 cm). Add allowances for draw-in, take-up, shrinkage, and loom waste.

Draw-in and **take-up** refer to the natural tendency of a weaving to be narrower and shorter than the warp due to interlacement. **Shrinkage** occurs when the finished fabric is washed and the yarns relax and contract some more.

We'll start by figuring the width of the warp and the number of warp ends. To end up with an 8-inch (20 cm) scarf, we must add extra width to allow for draw-in and shrinkage. A rough figure to add on is 10 percent, unless experience tells you differently. "Experience" comes from previous record sheets and from samples.

If we use the 10 percent figure, the total width of the warp for the scarf will need to be 8 plus .8 inches (20 plus 2 cm; gives an even 22 cm); this 8.8 inches can be rounded up to 9 inches. To find the number of warp ends to measure, multiply the width of the warp by the ends per inch or centimeter.

Desired finished width		8 inches	20 cm
Draw-in (approx. 10%)	+	1 inch	2 cm
Width of warp		9 inches	22 cm
Ends per inch/centimeter	×	10 inches	40/10
Total warp ends		90	88

Next we'll figure the length of the warp. To end up with a finished length of 54 inches (135 cm), we need to add an allowance for take-up, shrinkage, and loom waste. Again, a general figure for take-up is 10 percent, unless experience tells you differently. **Loom waste** is the amount of warp which can't be woven—it is the part used to tie onto the front beam and the

part behind the heddle which attaches the warp to the back beam. On most rigid heddle looms, 18 inches (45 cm) is a generous amount of loom waste. We don't need to add anything extra for fringe; that can come out of the loom waste.

Desired finished length	54 inches	135 cm
Take-up (approx. 10%)	5 inches	13.5
Loom waste (18″/45 cm) +	18 inches	45 cm
Warp length	77 inches	193.5 cm

This figure is 5 inches more than 2 yards (almost 195 cm); to wind the warp, find a path around your warping board (or set your warping pegs) to produce just over 2 yards (approximately 195 cm) of warp length.

To find out how much *warp yarn* to buy, multiply the number of warp ends by the length of the warp.

Number of warp ends	90 ends	88 ends
Length of warp ×	2.14 yds	195 cm
	195 yards	171.6 m

A series of pieces can be woven on one warp; when you are figuring the take-up and loom waste, add extra warp between the pieces to allow for fringe, hems, or other finishing. Then figure your total warp length and complete your calculations.

In a balanced weave, you will need slightly less yardage for the weft than you used for the warp. For balanced plain weave, you won't run out of weft if you buy the same amount of weft yarn as you buy of warp yarn. *As a rule of thumb, for a balanced weave you'll need about as much weft as warp.*

Compare the number of yards of yarn in the skein, tube, or pound (m/kg) of the yarn you want to determine how much to buy. Fine yarns have lots of yards per pound; coarse yarns have few yards per pound.

Some weaving yarns are labeled with numbers which tell how fine each component strand is and how many strands have been plied together to make the yarn (like 20/2, 8/4, or 1 ½ lea). The important thing to remember is that a higher count number (the first number in the equation) means a finer strand. The number of plies in a yarn is not an absolute guarantee of its strength, although frequently yarns with several plies are stronger than yarns with one or two. You will soon get to know the relative yarn sizes that are appropriate for the rigid heddle loom. Textured

---

[1]The slight discrepancy between the metric and U.S. Customary/British Imperial results occurred because we rounded up the 8.8 inches to 9. Two threads either way will not make a major difference in the scarf.

RECORD SHEET

Project _____

Warp yarn _____ _____ yds/tube or skein _____ yds/pound
(m/tube or skein) (m/kg)

_____ _____ _____

Weft yarn _____ _____ yds/tube or skein _____ yds/pound
(m/tube or skein) (m/kg)

_____ _____ _____

Heddle size _____

NUMBER OF WARP YARNS

Width of project _____ (inches/cm)

Draw-in and Shrinkage (10%) + _____

Total width on loom _____

Sett × _____ (EPI or ends/cm)

Number of warp yarns _____

YARN REQUIREMENTS

Warp: Length _____ inches _____ cm

Take-up and
shrinkage (10%) + _____ + _____

Loom waste + __18__ inches + __45__ cm

Total length in
inches/cm _____ inches _____ cm

÷ __36__ ÷ __100__

Total warp length
in yards/m _____ yards _____ m

Number of ends × _____ × _____

Amount needed _____ yards _____ m

Weft: Width _____ _____

Weft rows × _____ per inch _____ per cm

Weft yarn required _____ per woven inch _____ per woven cm

Length of project × _____ inches _____ cm

Total weft required
in inches/cm _____ inches _____ cm

÷ __36__ ÷ __100__

Total weft required
in yards/m _____ yards _____ m

EVALUATION of shrinkage, take-up/draw-in, and loom waste:

	width	length
On loom	_____	_____
Off loom	_____	_____
Washed	_____	_____

and knitting yarns do not have count numbers. It is more important to know how many yards there are in a skein, tube, or pound (m/kg), so you will know how much to buy to complete a project. Even if the yarn you are thinking about is not labeled, the shop may have a table which will give you yardage. Don't be afraid to ask.

Evaluation = help for future planning

Weave your scarf. When you are through, you can check your figures and gather information which will help you in future planning. The amount of unwoven warp (at the beginning and end of the project) is loom waste. Measure it and you will know how much to add as loom waste on *this* loom. This figure will be useful with every warp you measure for this particular loom. To figure the take-up, which applies to the type of yarn, weave, and sett which you used on this project, subtract the waste from the original warp length and compare the resulting number to the length of the finished scarf.

Warp length	2 yards 5 inches	195 cm
Loom waste (example)	19 inches	47.5 cm
Warp length used in scarf	1 yard 22 inches (58 inches)	147.5 cm

If your finished scarf measured 53 inches (132.5 cm) in length, then the take-up figure of 10 percent (5 inches/13.5 cm) was reasonably accurate. The loom waste on this imaginary loom was an inch *more* than on most rigid heddle looms, so the scarf is an inch (2.5 cm) shorter than you intended. You can wear and enjoy it, nonetheless, and will add 19 inches (47.5 cm) as your loom waste figure on future projects. If the take-up had varied from the estimate, you would revise your future figures accordingly.

Keep track of what happens each time you weave. You will understand the importance of these calculations the first time a warp isn't long enough to finish a project; if you keep careful records, you may avoid that problem!

CALCULATING AMOUNTS OF WEFT NEEDED

Under many circumstances, you can buy as much yarn for weft as you bought for warp. There may be times, however, when you want to figure out precisely how much weft you will need. The formula for doing this can be valuable in figuring weft requirements for warp- or weft-faced fabrics. You'll have to do a reasonably accurate sample to find out how many rows per inch your yarn com-bination requires. Then haul out the calculator and go to it.

You will multiply the width of the fabric by the number of weft rows per inch to get the amount of yarn required to weave 1 inch of fabric, and then multiply the result by the number of inches to be woven. Divide the result by 36 to get the number of yards you need.

Width of weaving	9 inches	24 cm
Rows	× 10 per inch	× 40/10 cm
Yarn used to weave 1″/10 cm of fabric	90 inches*	96 cm
Length to be woven	× 54 inches	× 135 cm
Amount of weft yarn in completed fabric	4860 inches	12960 cm
Yards/meters	÷ 36	÷ 100
Weft needed	135 yards	130 m

As a shortcut, you can stop at * and multiply the number of inches needed to weave 1 inch by the length of the completed fabric *in yards* (convert the 54 inches on the next line to 1.5 yards).

Yarn used to weave 1″ of fabric	90 inches
Amount to be woven, in yards	1.6 yards
Weft needed	135 yards

Warping Variations

Wide warps

It's easier to maintain even tension on wide warps if you wind several narrow warp chains. If a warp chain is too wide, the outer warps will wind on more tightly than the center warps. Making smaller chains also makes it easier to produce evenly tensioned warp ends of equal lengths; if you wind too many ends at one time on a warping board, the pegs will pull together under the tension and the last warp ends you wind will be shorter than the first.

Divide the total number of ends into several equal divisions, each of which should not contain more ends than will constitute 4 or 5 inches (10 to 12.5 cm) of width in the heddle. A 20-inch-wide (50 cm) warp, for instance, would be made into four warp chains. The narrower groupings wind more evenly onto the back beam than wide chains.

A wide warp will be hard to tension evenly.

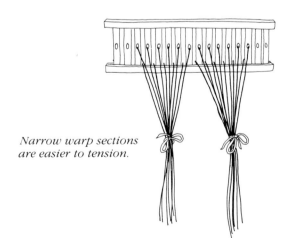

Narrow warp sections are easier to tension.

Speed warping

You will cut your warping time almost in half if you measure and thread two ends at a time. Use two cones or balls of yarn and you will need to make only half as many passes on the warping board. You will need some way to keep these two yarns from twisting around each other as you work; place them in separate boxes, and place a finger between the strands to keep them separated while you wind them onto the warping board. Divide the total number of ends needed by two to get the number of passes to make on the warping board, then divide this number into equal groups for the smaller warp chains described in the previous paragraph.

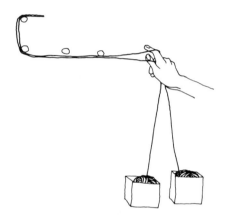

When you lift the first warp cross loop off your hand to thread the heddle, you will find yourself holding two loops wound as one. Separate the loops, pull each one through a separate slot, and carry both loops back together on the hook and attach them to the back beam.

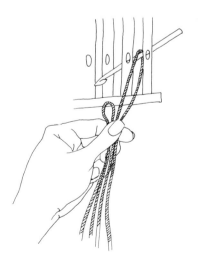

Three or four ends can be measured at a time and threaded in this manner, and you will further cut down on the time required to warp the loom. Each loop will be threaded through a separate slot.

If you are using two strands of a fine yarn as one warp end, you can measure the two yarns simultaneously as described above. When the time comes to separate the warp cross loops, pull the first loop through a slot and the next through a hole. Continue across; the threading of the heddle will be completed in one step—after you have beamed the warp you will be ready to tie onto the front beam and start weaving.

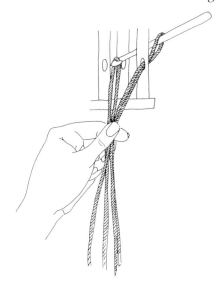

Warping back-to-front

In the first project, you learned the "back-to-front" method of warping. In this method, the warp loops at the cross were threaded only through the slots and then were attached to the back beam. Once the warp was rolled onto the back beam, one warp end was pulled out of each slot and threaded through an adjacent hole. This method maintains the relationships between the warps which were established on the warping board and avoids lumpy knots at the back.

Warping front-to-back

In the "front-to-back" method, the warp ends are cut at the end closest to the cross. The advantage to this method is that colors don't have to be kept in a particular order while the warp is wound; a chain can be made for each color and the colors can be put where you want them when you thread through the heddle. If you played with the random stripes under

"Discovering Plain Weave," you've already encountered this method.

Place the warp cross on your hand as usual. Instead of removing the bow tie at the end, slide it around to the side near the cross. Insert a scissor blade through all the end loops and cut them. *Be sure to cut at the center of the loops so the ends are all the same length.* Remove the warp ends one at a time and thread them through the holes and slots.

Tie ½-inch groups of warp ends with overhand knots and slip them over the pegs or dowel rod on the warp beam. Be careful when you tie the warp groups that the knots all occur at the same distance from the cut ends, so each group will be the same length as the others. If one group is longer or shorter, you will spend time adjusting that difference throughout the whole warp chain. Place heavy paper over the knots to provide a smooth surface over which the warp will wind.

When you are ready to fasten the warp ends to the front beam, tie them in 1-inch groups and lash them on.

Working with finer yarns

When weaving with a rigid heddle loom, we have to choose the yarn to fit the size of the heddle. There are, however, several ways to use a fine yarn with a rigid heddle.

We've discussed using the yarn doubled in the warp and in the weft. Threaded in a 10-dent (40/10) heddle, there will be 20 warps per inch (80/10). However, since two strands work as one, there are still only 10 working ends per inch (40/10), and the doubled weft should be beaten in at 10 wefts per inch (4/cm) for a balanced fabric. This weave structure (two-over-two) is known as *basket weave*. It makes a lighter weight fabric than one woven with a heavier yarn at the same sett. A lighter and more drapable fabric can be woven by using a single strand for the weft over a doubled warp, with between 15 and 20 weft shots per inch (6 to 8/cm).

Another way is to thread the warp with a single strand in each hole and two strands together in each slot. With this threading there will be 15 warps per inch (60/10), but still only 10 working ends per inch (4/cm). A single strand is used for the weft at 15 picks per inch (6/cm) for balanced weave. The surface texture is rough, because of the thick and thin warp units. The hand is light and drapable.

If your loom lets you use more than one heddle at once, however, you can use two identical heddles and thread them according to a pattern which will give you more threads to the inch than the single heddle allows. The chart of rigid heddle looms at the beginning of this book gives an indication of which looms can be used with multiple heddles. Loom designs change, and home ingenuity may provide a solution to this problem if you have a loom which is at first glance not appropriate.

Two identical 10-dent (40/10) heddles can be threaded to give 20 EPI (80/10) or 15 EPI (60/10). Two 12-dent (48/10) heddles can be threaded for 24 EPI or 18 EPI.

Having this capacity allows you to use a much wider range of yarns and to weave finer fabrics than you can produce with one heddle. Another reason to use multiple heddles is for more complex techniques which are beyond the scope of this book; however, using two heddles to increase the density of your sett will help you become familiar with the use of extra heddles in preparation for exploring those techniques.

Threading two heddles

The illustration shows how the warp ends are threaded through two heddles to produce different setts. To weave plain weave with this system, you will hold the two heddles together as you raise and lower them to make the sheds. Use only the front heddle to beat the weft into place.

Threading two rigid heddles at once is not complicated if you approach it methodically. The *heddle holder* is a very important aid to threading two heddles simultaneously. Most looms provide some support for one heddle during threading, but few offer a place to put a second heddle. You will be frustrated if the heddles slip or fall over as you try to thread them, so use a C-clamp or make a special holder to keep the extra heddle upright.

Heddle holders

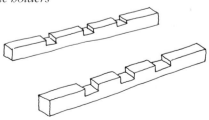

This silk scarf was woven at 20 E.P.I., using two 10-dent heddles. The two-ply silk at 4400 yd/lb was embellished with an inlay in variegated rayon chenille on every fourth row.

It also helps to mark each heddle at 1-inch intervals, as described under "Preparations" for the first project. This will make it simpler to center the warp and to align the two heddles. For the first few times, I recommend that you use the front-to-back warping method and cut the warp loops at the cross before you thread the heddles.

For twice as many warps per inch. Two 10-dent heddles will give 20 ends per inch, two 8-dent heddles will give 16 ends per inch, and two 12-dent heddles will give 24 ends per inch.

Begin by removing the first four warps from the warp cross.

(1) Pick up the first two warps and thread them into the first heddle, one through a hole and one through the slot to its left.

Then pull both of these ends through the slot to the right of the equivalent hole in the second heddle; the 1-inch markings on the heddles will help you identify the appropriate slot on the second heddle.

(2) Pick up the other two warps and thread them through the same slot you just used on the first heddle.

In the second heddle, pull one end through the hole to the left of the slot you used for the previous pair and the other through the slot to its left.

Threading two heddles for twice as many warps per inch.

This completes one repeat of the threading sequence. If you remove from the cross only the number of warps needed for one threading repeat (four), you will always know where you are in the sequence.

After you complete each sequence, make a quick check to be sure there is a warp in each hole and three warps in each slot of both heddles. The fourth thread of each repeat should line up in the equivalent slots of both heddles. Even up the ends, tie the group in an overhand knot, and attach it to the back beam (slip over pegs or dowel rod).

For one-and-one-half times as many warps per inch. Two 10-dent heddles will give 15 ends per inch, two 8-dent heddles will give 12 ends per inch, and two 12-dent heddles will give 18 ends per inch.

The threading has six warp ends in each repeat.

(1) Remove six warps from the cross. Pick up the first three. Thread one through a hole and the other two through the slot to the left.

In the second heddle, thread the first two of these ends through the slot to the right of the hole which matches the hole you used on the first heddle and thread the third end through the matching hole.

(2) Pick up the other three ends. Thread one through the same slot on the first heddle that you used for the last batch, one through the next hole to its left, and the last one through the slot to the left of the hole.

In the second heddle, the first two ends go through the slot which matches the one you started with on the first heddle and the third through the slot to its left. The hole remains empty.

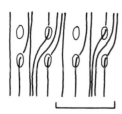

Threading two heddles for one-and-one-half times as many warps per inch.

Make a quick check to see that there is a warp in every hole of the first heddle, and one in every other hole of the second heddle. In the slots of both heddles there should be three warps and one warp alternating. As each repeat is threaded, tie that group with an overhand knot and attach to the back beam.

Weaving at finer setts

For a balanced weave with 20 ends per inch (80/10) you use 20 wefts per inch (8/cm). If the sett of the yarn is for a firm weave, it will be difficult to beat the weft down tightly enough to make a balanced fabric with the threading for twice as many warps, because of the uneven spacing of the warp. As the heddle is brought forward to beat the weft in, the plastic teeth squeeze together the three warps in each slot on the front heddle. You'll find that if you use a weft slightly finer than the warp you'll be able to beat it in at 20 wefts per inch (8/cm).

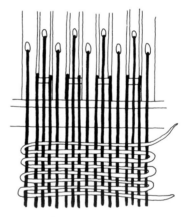

When two heddles are used for finer setts, a true plain weave is produced but the grouping of threads in the slots may make the cloth look streaky. This may or may not be a problem.

The uneven spacing causes streaks in the cloth, which may or may not disappear with washing. The fabric has a nice, lightweight, crisp hand with faint vertical stripes.

If you use the second threading with two 10-dent heddles to get 15 EPI, the weft should be beaten to 15 EPI for a balanced fabric. The spacing of the warp ends in this threading is also uneven. The streaks are more prominent than those in the previous threading pattern and they don't usually wash out. They can be considered part of the fabric design, or they can be disguised by the use of a striped warp. Very narrow stripes work especially well. The fabric is lightweight and has a nice, drapable hand.

98

GETTING THE MOST FROM YOUR RIGID HEDDLE LOOM

Threadings for a variety of setts:
(brackets indicate one repeat).

Heddle size	8	10	12
		Ends per inch	

ONE HEDDLE

½ as many warps per inch

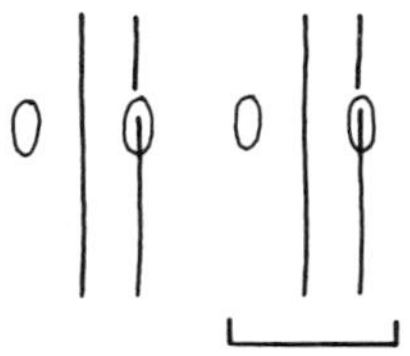

	4	5	6

regular threading

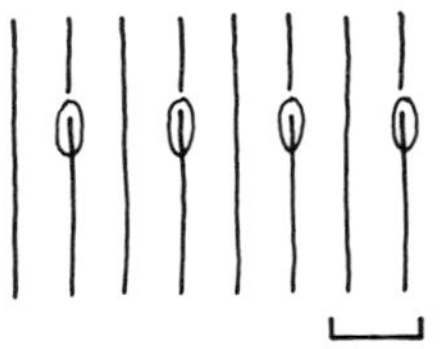

	8	10	12

TWO HEDDLES

1½ times as many warps per inch

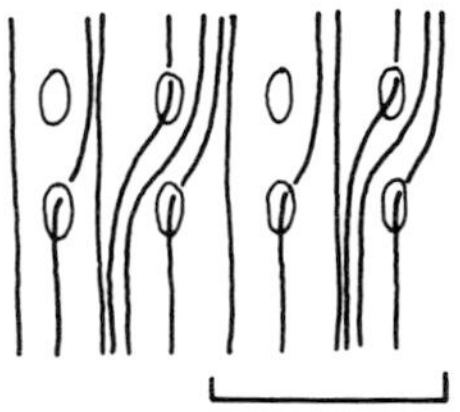

	12	15	18

2 times as many warps per inch

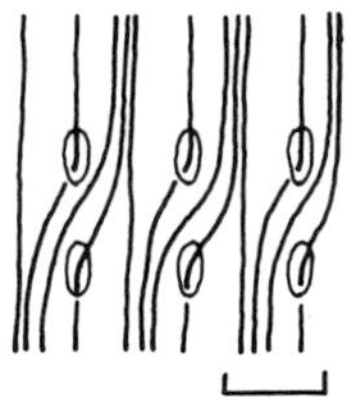

	16	20	24

How to read these diagrams. The lower row of holes represents the heddle closest to the front of the loom. The spaces between the holes are the slots in that heddle.

The upper row of holes represents the heddle toward the back of the loom. The spaces between are the slots in that heddle.

A single threading repeat is bracketed, but more than one repeat is pictured so you can see the pattern.

As an example, in the bottom diagram the first thread goes through the first hole in heddle one and the first slot to the right of the corresponding hole in heddle two.

The other three threads in the repeat all pass through the slot just to the left of the hole already used in heddle one. However, they go into different places in heddle two.

The second thread goes through the slot to the *right* of the hole which corresponds to the hole already used in heddle one (marking your heddle helps a lot!). The third thread goes through the hole which matches the filled hole in heddle one. The fourth thread goes in the slot to the left of that hole; this slot will also be used for the first two threads of the next repeat.

This type of threading is easier to do than to talk about!

Blue Cotton Top

Designed by Betty Davenport

FABRIC DESCRIPTION: Plain weave.

SIZE: Women's large; circumference at chest 46″ (115 cm), length from shoulder 20½″ (51.25 cm).

WARP & WEFT: 3/2 pearl cotton at 1260 yd/lb (2523 m/kg): 1150 yd (1046 m) medium blue, 70 yds (64 m) bright green, 84 yds (77 m) dark purple, and 25 yds (23 m) rust.

E.P.I.: 12 (48/10 cm).

HEDDLE: 12-dent (48/10).

WIDTH IN HEDDLE: 14″ (35.2 cm).

TOTAL WARP ENDS: 169.

WARP LENGTH: 4 yd (3.6 m), which includes shrinkage, take-up, and 18″ (45 cm) loom waste.

WEFT ROWS PER INCH: 12 (48/10 cm).

WEAVING: With medium blue, weave plain weave to end of warp.

FINISHING: Machine wash and dry. Iron while still slightly damp.

ASSEMBLY: Machine zigzag on each side of cutting lines before cutting fabric. Cut a 22″ (55 cm) length for the sleeves. Cut this piece in half lengthwise for the two sleeve pieces. Fold the remaining fabric in half and cut. Join the two pieces at the center seam. Cover the seam line with a lacing stitch using dark purple.

Mark the neckline with a basting thread. Zigzag twice around the neck edge before cutting away the excess fabric. Lay three strands of dark purple yarn around the neck edge, and with medium blue work a row of single crochet over them to cover the machine stitching. To angle the shoulder line, sew shoulder darts 1″ (2.5 cm) deep at selvedge edge tapering to nothing at the neck opening.

Center a sleeve piece at the shoulderline, stretching it slightly to ease the fabric over the shoulder. Pin in place, join and finish the selvedges the same as the center seam. Turn up and press the sleeve hem. Stitch the side seam from bottom to top, continuing across the end of the sleeve at an angle, pivoting at the fold line and angling back to the edge. Hand hem the sleeve seam on the inside. Turn under a hem at the lower edge. □

WARP COLOR ORDER:

Medium blue	2			1		1		1		6		1				1		25		25
Bright green		1	1						3						3					1
Rust			1										1	1						
Dark purple				2	2	2	2						1				1			

↑ center
← Reverse from center

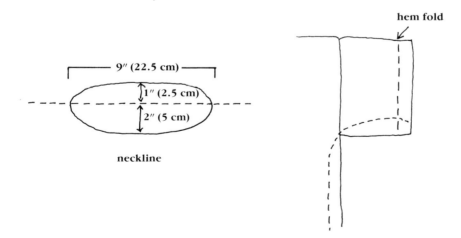

sleeve

sleeve

left front and back

right front and back

14″ (35 cm)

22″ (55 cm)   44″ (110 cm)   44″ (110 cm)

9″ (22.5 cm)

1″ (2.5 cm)

2″ (5 cm)

neckline

hem fold

angling sleeve seam

A handful of colors of pearl cotton in a striped warp are crossed by a one-color weft and embellished with a seam detail in this comfortable, cheerful blouse.

Shuttles for weaving with finer yarns.
Winding fine yarns onto a stick shuttle becomes
tedious. *Boat shuttles,* which carry bobbins of
yarn, were designed for fine yarns. Some boat
shuttles are shallow enough to fit through the
shed on a rigid heddle loom. Swedish boat
shuttles, only ¾ inch (2 cm) thick, work well.
You'll need a supply of bobbins and a *bobbin
winder,* to make filling them easy.

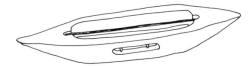

A boat shuttle

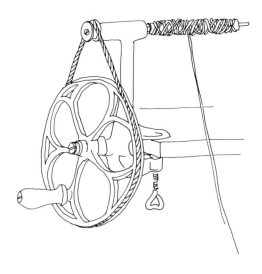

A bobbin winder

In the End

When you cut your project off the loom, you
can breathe in satisfaction, but you are not quite
done. The warp ends must be secured, the fringe
must be treated in some way, and the whole
piece will probably need to be washed and
pressed. The first project introduced you to
some of the possibilities for completing a weaving. There are many other choices which you
can consider.

Securing warp ends

Overhand knots. The overhand knots you
used in the first project are secure and simple.
Make a fringe with them, or knot the fabric into
a tube for a pillow or a tote bag, with the
method described in the section on the tote bag
project.

Gathering knot. The gathering knot is an
overhand knot tied with one strand around a
group of warps. Separate one of the ends, loop it
around the rest, bring its tail through the loop,
and tighten it. Your knot will be less obvious if
you make it with only one strand in this way.

Gathering knot

Hemstitching. To get a flat, secure finish
without the bumps of knots, try hemstitching.
You can do the stitching with the yarn you used
as warp or weft or with a finer yarn. Hemstitching done with sewing thread is nearly invisible.

Hemstitching the beginning of a piece

Hemstitching the end of a piece

Measure a strand three times as long as your weaving is wide. Thread it through a blunt needle. Work from either side; this description and the diagrams begin from the left side. Secure the end by needleweaving it in along the last weft shot. Then insert the needle four warps over. Bring the yarn under and up, around the four warps. Then take the needle down under two weft threads, as shown in the diagram. Continue this stitch across the fabric and secure the final end of the yarn by needleweaving it in along the last weft shot.

Hemstitching can be done around as few as two warps, but should not span more than ½ inch (1.25 cm) of warp ends.

If you know ahead of time that you will finish your piece with hemstitching, you can do the needlework while the weaving is on the loom. When you weave your first weft pick, leave a length of yarn extending from the left side that is three times the width of the weaving. After you have woven about an inch (2.5 cm), work the hemstitching along the beginning edge with the length of yarn hanging from the left side. After you finish your weaving, leave another length of weft hanging from the left this time, and hemstitch the piece before removing it from the loom.

Trimming fringe evenly. To make sure you cut fringe evenly, lay the weaving on a table with its end parallel to the table edge. Smooth out the fringe and cut it with sharp scissors, using the table edge as a guideline.

Weaving in the ends. Sometimes you may not want any warp ends to show beyond the ends of your piece. Each end can be threaded into a needle and drawn up along the warp next to it for about an inch (2.5 cm). If you know you will be using this finish, you can lay in the first and last inches (centimeters) of weft shots a little loosely to leave space for the extra thickness of the doubled warps. This is a very neat way to finish a weft-faced piece.

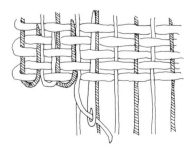

Machine stitching cut edges. If the ends of your fabric are to be hemmed or sewn into a seam, the warps may be secured with machine stitching. Zigzag along a single weft pick, so your stitching will be straight. Sew a second row that slightly overlaps the first. If you don't have a zigzag setting, you can use two rows of straight stitching. If you intend to cut the fabric into shapes or curves, stitch the edges to secure them before you cut. If you cut your fabric into two pieces, stitch on both sides of the cutting line before you snip.

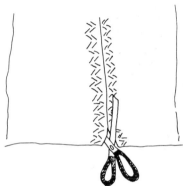

Hems

Sometimes it's nice to weave hem allowances with a yarn which matches your weft in color but is finer in size, to reduce bulk. This is an especially useful trick for heavy place mats. Zigzag the edge on a sewing machine and trim the warp ends close to the stitching. Turn up the edge twice—to hide the machine stitching and the rough edge—and slipstitch the hem by hand. If the hem is much too bulky when you turn it up twice, you can turn it up once and use the catch stitch to hem it.

Slip stitch

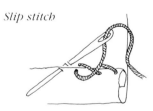

Catch stitch

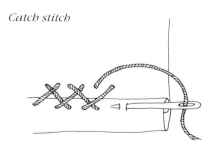

Made in panels, this afghan can be produced on a narrow loom. It's soft and warm: perfect to keep handy for snuggling.

Purple Afghan

Designed by Betty Davenport

FABRIC DESCRIPTION: Plain weave with weft float patterns.

FINISHED DIMENSIONS: Five panels sewn together to make 47½″ (119 cm) wide × 74″ (185 cm) long plus 1¼″ (3 cm) fringe on each end.

WARP: 12/3 worsted wool at 2160 yd/lb (4325 m/kg). This is Nehalem from Oregon Worsted, available on 270 yd (246 m)/8 oz tubes: 5 tubes Purple (some used for weft).

WEFT: Some of the above, plus 2-ply wool at 1400 yd/lb (2800 m/kg): 1000 yd (910 m) grape heather, 525 yd (478 m) purple heather, small amounts of bright purple, blue heather, and teal.

E.P.I.: 10 (40/10 cm).

HEDDLE: 10-dent (40/10).

WIDTH IN HEDDLE: 10″ (25 cm) for each warp.

TOTAL WARP ENDS: 100 in each warp chain.

WARP LENGTH: 2 warp chains, each 5 yards (4.5 m) long, and 1 warp chain 2½ yards (2.25 m) long.

WEFT ROWS PER INCH: 8 (32/10 cm).

TAKE-UP & SHRINKAGE: 10% in width and length.

WEAVING: Each of the five panels starts with border stripes and has five blocks of solid grape and random stripes alternated. The border stripes are not repeated at the ends of the panels. Two of the panels have the solid and striped blocks in reverse order. To make sure each strip matches, mark the measurements for the pattern changes on a template and pin it along the selvedge of the weaving as you work.

For the border of each panel, weave 1″ (2.5 cm) stripes in grape, purple heather, teal, grape, purple heather. The third and fourth stripes are woven with a pattern, using one color in the plain weave shed and a different color in the pattern shed. For the pattern, pick up as follows: 3 up (2 down, 1 up, 2 down, 1 up, 2 down, 4 up, repeated across), end with 3 up. Weave plain weave up shed, pattern stick shed, plain weave down shed, pattern stick shed, repeated.

For the middle of the panel, weave 14½″ (36 cm) blocks alternately in solid grape and in stripes of random widths. Occasionally, weave some weft float pattern in bright purple, blue, or teal for variety and texture.

ASSEMBLY: Lay the panels side by side. Pin the first two strips together so the pattern matches. Join the selvedges of the panels with the invisible stitch or whipstitch. Join the other panels in the same manner.

FINISHING: It is best to wash and press the afghan after it has been assembled. Hand wash gently or use the washing machine without agitation. Smooth out on a flat surface to dry. Steam press. □

Crocheted or knitted trim

Added trim can enhance weaving. To prepare the edge of your fabric, machine stitch the edge. A stronger, smoother edge will result if you turn the fabric under ¼ inch and then machine stitch.

Work a row of single crochet over the edge. Work additional rows of crochet as desired. Knitting stitches can be picked up on a needle from the base row of crochet and then worked in ribbing. See crochet and knitting books for more ideas.

A base of single crochet allows you to add more elaborate trims, or may be sufficient in itself.

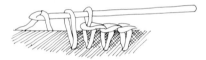

Protecting fringe

Sometimes fringe will need further treatment to protect it from fraying or to make it more decorative.

Twisted fringe. Divide the strands in an overhand knot into two groups. Take a close look to determine the direction of the twist in the yarn. Start with a group in each hand; work both groups at the same time. Twist each group in the direction of its original twist until it is tight and starts to kink. Put the free ends of the two strands together and twist them in the other direction. Secure the end with a gathering knot.

Braiding. Warp ends can also be worked into a variety of different braids. The simplest way is to divide the warp ends which you want to braid into three groups and braid them as you would in making a pigtail. Secure the end of the braid with an overhand knot.

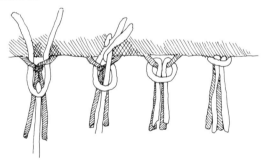

Adding extra fringe. If your warp ends look skimpy or you want them to have more importance on your final piece, add more strands of yarn. Fringe can be applied to a selvedge in the same way, if you want fringe all the way around a piece.

Cut lengths of yarn that are a little more than double the desired length of your fringe. Lay several strands together and fold them in half. Pull the end loop through the center of the existing fringe knot or through the selvedge with a crochet hook. Bring the ends of the extra strands through the loop and pull them to tighten it.

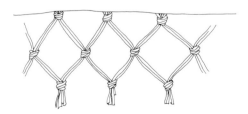

A decorative finish. Divide the strands of two adjoining knotted groups into halves. Tie a second row of knots, joining the adjacent halves of the neighboring groups with an overhand knot. Repeat across the fabric. Do a third row of knots, joining the halves back with their original groups, making a diamond pattern. Use the gathering knot for a flat finish.

Joining panels

The way you join panels together can be decorative or nearly invisible. Joining panels allows you to weave projects much larger than your loom and expands your possibilities for creating big patterns.

Invisible stitch. Thread a length of the warp yarn into a blunt needle. Stitch alternately through a weft loop on one side, then one on the other side. Draw the stitching yarn up tight.

This seam is particularly invisible if the needle is inserted into the weft loop in a direction opposite to that followed by the outside warp. This makes the stitching yarn interweave with the fabric as if it were another warp end. Look at the illustration carefully to see what is happening.

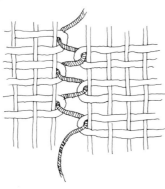

Whip stitch. This is an overcasting stitch. Lay the two pieces of fabric back-to-back and whip over the selvedges. This stitch produces a slightly raised ridge along the seam; the subtly textured effect could be just what your weaving needs.

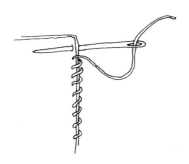

Lacing. This technique provides surface decoration and makes a very flexible seam. Butt the edges of two fabrics (lay them flat, with their selvedges touching). Stitch into each fabric in turn, putting your needle through it several warps in from the edge.

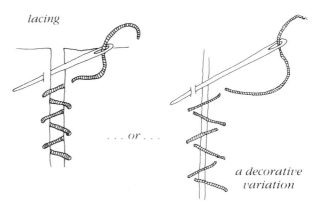

lacing

. . . or . . .

a decorative variation

Machine stitching. To stitch two edges together by machine, butt their edges and stitch over them with a wide machine zigzag stitch. Cover the machine stitching by couching several yarns over it. To couch yarns in place, you lay them on the surface of the fabric where you want them to be secured and make small, even stitches across them at regular intervals. The stitches should be no more than ½ inch (1.25 cm) apart.

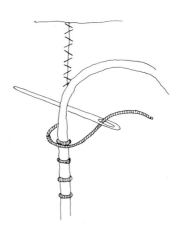

Fabric finishing

Warp- and weft-faced weaves usually need only a good steam pressing, and wall hangings and rugs can be fastened to a flat surface in the desired shape and steam pressed to straighten their edges. Washing makes the greatest difference for balanced weaves; washing improves many handwoven fabrics considerably. The spinning oils are removed, the yarns relax and expand, and the weave structure is set into place. Some fabrics look awful coming off the loom but assume wonderful textures once they have been washed.

Washing. Cotton and linen fabrics which you would like to be able to wash easily should be run through the washer and dryer before you cut or sew them. With linen, you can choose whether you'd like your finished weaving to retain its initial stiffness or to have a soft, drapable hand. The washing machine will soften the fibers; if you want them crisper, hand wash the fabric with the method described below and don't put them in the dryer.

Remove machine-washed fabric from the dryer while it is still damp and smooth it out on a flat surface. Iron directly on cottons and linens while they are still slightly damp. If you let them dry before ironing them, the wrinkles will be hard to get out. After being washed a few times, many cottons and cotton/linen blends will no longer need to be ironed. Unbleached fibers will lighten with each washing in regular laundry detergents or soaps. To preserve the natural shades longer, wash fabrics made of unbleached fibers by hand in mild soap.

You may want to maintain the body of linen fabrics, especially in decorative pieces woven with the openwork techniques. Hand wash them without squeezing. Rinse well and roll in a towel to extract the water. Do not wring them out. Smooth the fabric flat to dry and iron it while it's still slightly damp.

Silk fabrics should be hand washed in warm water with a mild liquid detergent. Roll the clean fabric on a towel to extract the excess water and then smooth it out on a flat surface to dry. Iron it while it is still slightly damp.

Wool items also appreciate being hand washed in warm water with mild liquid detergent or soap. Use the towel procedure to extract the water or put them in the SPIN ONLY cycle of a washing machine. Smooth them out on a flat surface to dry. Press with a damp cloth and a steam iron while the fabric is just barely damp.

Fulling. Some wonderful things can happen to wool fabrics when they are machine washed *once*, as part of the finishing process. If the woolen fabric has been loosely woven, the yarns will fluff up and shrink, leaving a wonderfully soft and stable fabric appropriate for outerwear garments. A tightly woven fabric may turn into something which resembles a board. Machine washing of woolens should be approached with caution, and you should experiment with several samples to see how the yarns react before you throw your valuable yardage in the machine.

When you want to "full" a woolen fabric in the washing machine, use hot water and laundry detergent. Washing action can last from a few minutes to fifteen minutes or more; stop the machine periodically to check the condition of the fabric. If you carry this process too far, you will end up with a little piece of felt.

As soon as the fabric has the texture and finish you want, rinse it gently in clear water similar in temperature to the washing water, spin it to get the water out, and either lay it flat to dry or use a dryer on low heat until it is just damp. Press as usual for wool.

Fulling is done only once. Future cleaning should be done by hand washing or dry cleaning.

Steam pressing. Lay a damp cloth over the fabric. Press with a hot iron until the pressing cloth stops sizzling. Lift the iron and move it to the next spot. Let the steam dissipate before you move the cloth to the next area.

Brushing. For a very soft and fluffy fabric, you can brush the surface with a stiff brush. Brushing brings the wool fibers to the surface, giving a furry surface that increases the fabric's insulating power and softens its colors. Brushing is especially nice for wool scarves, stoles, and blankets. An ironing board makes a convenient work surface, since it can be adjusted to a comfortable height, but a table or your lap will also work. Use a laundry brush, hairbrush, or other tool, with either natural or nylon bristles. Brush the fabric while it is still damp, since the fibers will come to the surface more easily. Use a light, uplifting motion, moving gently across the surface. Use only three or four strokes in an area. Too much brushing will give you a very shaggy piece of cloth. You can brush one or both sides, depending on the use to which the fabric will be put.

Appendix

The Portable Loom

Some rigid heddle looms have been designed so you can take them apart and carry them elsewhere while they are warped. Disassemble the loom and roll it up like this:

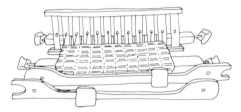

Then take to the road!

If you plan to carry your loom to workshops or on trips, a loom tote bag, which you can make from sturdy handwoven fabric or from commercial fabric, will make it extremely portable.

The plans here fit my 20-inch (50 cm) loom. Make sure that your finished tote bag will be wide and deep enough for your assembled loom.

1. Cut fabric according to plan. Make sure that the measurement from A to B is long enough: measure the depth of your loom plus 5 inches (25 cm) for seams and box corners plus 2 or 3 inches (5 to 7.5 cm) of ease. The sizes of the pocket and strap can vary, depending on how much fabric is left.

2. Turn under ¼ inch (.75 cm) on all four edges of the pocket piece; press. On one long edge, turn under a hem allowance (at least ½ inch/1.25 cm), press, and stitch down. Place the pocket on the large piece of fabric and stitch it into position on the three unhemmed sides.

3. Hem the large piece of fabric along lines A-B as you did the pocket. Fold and stitch the straps as noted on diagram, then stitch the straps in place.

4. Fold the large piece of fabric in half, right sides together, along line C-C. Pin together side edges and stitch in a ½-inch (1.25 cm) seam.

5. Fold bottom corner and seam diagonally, as in diagram.

6. Turn tote bag right side out and admire!

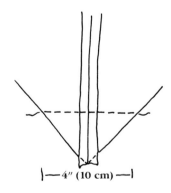

—4" (10 cm)—

Fold bottom corner so side seam matches bottom center line. Stitch across point to make box corner. Stitch corner point down to bottom.

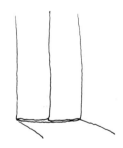

Corner on outside.

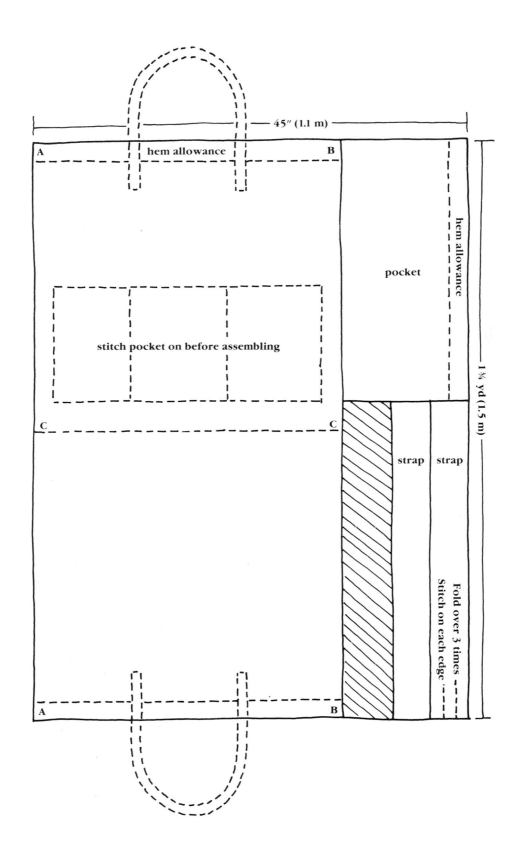

45″ (1.1 m)

A hem allowance B

pocket

hem allowance

stitch pocket on before assembling

C   C

strap strap

1¾ yd (1.5 m)

Fold over 3 times
Stitch on each edge

A   B

111

Troubleshooting

While winding the warp onto the back beam, you notice that one side of one warp chain has increasingly more loose ends than the other.

This happens because too much warp was wound on the warping board at one time. The pegs were pulled together by the pressure of the many warp ends and the part of the warp chain which you measured last is shorter than the first part.

To prevent this problem, wind fewer ends in each warp chain. It's best to make a separate warp chain for every 4 to 5 inches (10 to 12.5 cm) of the width of your weaving. This means you would make four warp chains for a 20-inch-wide (50 cm) weaving.

Shake and smooth the warp chain, working the looser warps down to the next choke-tie. It's important that all the warp ends maintain the same tension as they wind onto the back beam. Trim the cut ends even before you thread through the holes and tie onto the front beam.

One end of the heddle keeps falling off the shed block, in either the up shed or the down shed, or both.

This happens when the warp is not lined up absolutely straight, from the back beam through the heddle to the front beam. The warp is traveling that path at a slight angle and pulls the heddle out of line. If the problem is minor, you can live with it.

If it's driving you crazy, check the marks on the heddle and the beams to see where the warp goes out of alignment. If the problem is between the heddle and the front beam, it will straighten itself out as soon as you weave enough to wind some fabric around the front beam. As you wind it on, you can shift the fabric slightly to one side to line up the warp with the heddle and the back beam. If the crookedness occurs between the heddle and the back beam, you'll have falling heddle difficulties throughout the length of the warp. If you have just begun to weave, you may find it worthwhile to go back and rethread the heddle.

Prevent the problem by marking your heddle and your beams, and by using the marks during warping.

The tension loosens each time you beat the weft into place.

A little of this is normal in the first few inches of weaving, especially if you did not pull the warp tight every few revolutions when you wound it onto the back beam. In this case, the layers of paper and warp are just tightening around the back beam.

If the tension adjustment on your loom is controlled by wing-nuts, knobs, or threaded screws, rather than by a ratchet system, the tension will not hold securely if the screw threads are worn. The screw threads on the righthand side of the loom will wear out first and you may be able to solve the problem by rotating screws or threaded knobs from side to side or back to front. If that doesn't work, the threads are probably stripped. Replace the screw or, if the threads are on a rod extending from the end of the beam, the entire beam.

Unplanned skips or floats keep showing up in the woven fabric.

This can happen when the warp threads are crossed behind the heddle. Clear the shed behind the heddle with your fingers or a pick-up stick. You'll have to do this every time the warp is rolled forward.

A warp thread breaks!

Cut a length of mending warp about a yard long. Fasten a T-pin or a large straight pin to the fabric crosswise near the fell line and wind one end of the mending warp around it in a figure eight. Thread the other end through the heddle in the broken warp's location and tie it to the broken warp end at the back beam with a bow knot. Each time you roll the warp forward move the knot back out of the way, until the weaving has progressed far enough that the original warp can be pulled forward to overlap the woven cloth. At this point you can put another pin at the fell line and fasten the original warp end to it in a figure eight, as you did the mending warp. Continue to weave.

When you have taken the completed fabric off the loom, use a blunt needle to weave in each end of the mending warp so they overlap the original warp end by about an inch (2.5 cm) and trim off the tails of both pieces of yarn.

You find a knot in the warp.

Knots in the warp are usually too big to go through the heddle. Prevent this problem by removing any knots in the yarn while you measure your warp; back up to one end-peg or the other and make a knot there to keep your warping continuous. If you miss a knot and find it while you're weaving, untie it and treat it like a broken warp end.

After threading the loom, you find you have skipped a hole or slot which should contain a warp end.

Cut a piece of yarn the full length of your warp. Tie it to the front beam or, if you've already begun to weave, work one end into the woven cloth with a blunt needle and pin it into place. Pull the yarn through the skipped space in the heddle. Fasten a T-pin into the roll of warp on the back beam and wrap the yarn around the pin in a figure eight, adjusting its tension to match that of the rest of the warp. You'll have to refasten and readjust this pin each time you roll the warp forward.

There are two warps in a space which should contain one.

Check to see if any space is *missing* a warp. If so, your solution will depend on whether you've started weaving or not. If so, cut one of the extra warp ends near the front beam, pull it carefully out of the weaving, thread it correctly, needle-weave it into the fabric in the correct space, and pin its end to hold it in place. If not, you can untie the knot at the front beam which contains the misthreaded ends, thread them correctly, and retie.

If one of the warp ends truly appears to be "extra," cut it close to the fabric being woven, pull it toward the back and out of the heddle, and toss it over the back beam. Ignore it.

Your selvedges are uneven and you're being very careful with the way you put your weft into the shed.

Check to see if the tension on the edge warps feels looser than the tension on the rest of the warp. This can happen if the warp isn't wound evenly onto the back beam—if, for some reason, the paper or warp builds up too thickly on the edges of the warp—or if a shuttle has snagged the edge warps and stretched them.

You can increase the tension on the loose warp ends by stuffing a roll or wad of paper under the loose ends at the back beam. If you've only got one loose warp end, and it's *very* loose, pull the warp end *forward*, pin its "extra" length at the fell line of your fabric (like repairing a broken warp end), and repair the loop when the fabric is finished, by gently pulling it to the end of the fabric or by cutting it and weaving its two ends into the fabric so they overlap.

Bibliography and Resources

The techniques and ideas presented in this book are only the beginning of the possibilities for rigid heddle weavers. In addition to "just plain weave," which can be a satisfying long-term preoccupation in itself, the rigid heddle loom can easily produce a group of more complicated weaves. Some of these are presented in my monograph *Textures and Patterns for the Rigid Heddle Loom*. Additional challenging techniques expand the use of two and three heddles, which we have introduced here. With the use of multiple heddles, the rigid heddle loom can produce structures commonly woven on harness looms.

The books listed below will spur your imagination, whether you want to explore in greater depth the topics presented here or to dive into more intricate techniques.

Rigid heddle weaving

Davenport, Betty Linn. *Textures and Patterns for the Rigid Heddle Loom.* Saint Paul, Minn.: Dos Tejedoras, 1980.

-----. "Rigid Heddle Weaving, Level 1." Videotaped instruction. Port Townsend, Wash.: Victorian Video Productions, 1986.

McKinney, David B. *Weaving with Three Rigid Heddles.* Greenley Hill, Calif.: Mountain Gate Monastery, 1985.

Xenakis, David A. *The Xenakis Technique for the Construction of Four-Harness Textiles.* Sioux Falls, S.D.: Golden Fleece, 1978.

General Weaving

Baizerman, Suzanne, and Karen Searle. *Latin American Brocades: Explorations in Supplementary Weft Techniques.* Saint Paul, Minn.: Dos Tejedoras, 1976.

-----. *Finishes in the Ethnic Tradition.* Saint Paul, Minn.: Dos Tejedoras, 1978.

Beard, Betty J. *Fashions from the Loom.* Loveland, Colo.: Interweave Press, 1980.

Collingwood, Peter. *The Techniques of Rug Weaving.* New York: Watson-Guptill, 1968.

Harvey, Nancy. *The Guide to Successful Tapestry Weaving.* Seattle, Wash.: Pacific Search Press, 1981.

-----. *Patterns for Tapestry Weaving.* Seattle, Wash.: Pacific Search Press, 1984.

Mayer, Anita Luvera. *Clothing from the Hands That Weave.* Loveland, Colo.: Interweave Press, 1984.

Quinn, Celia. *Yarn: A Resource Guide for Handweavers.* Loveland, Colo.: Interweave Press, 1985.

Sutton, Ann. *Color-and-Weave Design.* Asheville, N.C.: Lark Communications, 1984.

Tidball, Harriet. *Brocade.* Shuttle Craft Guild Monograph 22. Coupeville, Wash.: HTH Publishers, 1967.

-----. *Contemporary Tapestry.* Shuttle Craft Guild Monograph 12. Coupeville, Wash.: HTH Publishers, 1964.

-----. *Two Harness Textiles: The Open-Work Weaves.* Shuttle Craft Guild Monograph 21. Coupeville, Wash.: HTH Publishers, 1967.

-----. *Weaving Inkle Bands.* Shuttle Craft Guild Monograph 27. Coupeville, Wash.: HTH Publishers, 1969.

Weavers Guild of Boston. *Processing and Finishing Handwoven Textiles.* Boston, Mass.: The Weavers Guild of Boston, 1980.

Wilson, Jean. *Weaving is Creative.* New York: Van Nostrand Reinhold, 1972.

Design and color

Birren, Faber, ed. *A Grammar of Color: A Basic Treatise on the Color System of Munsell.* New York: Van Nostrand Reinhold, 1969.

Birren, Faber. *The Textile Colorist.* New York: Van Nostrand Reinhold, 1980.

de Sausmarez, Maurice. *Basic Design: The Dynamics of Visual Form.* New York: Van Nostrand Reinhold, 1964.

Edwards, Edward B. *Pattern and Design with Dynamic Symmetry.* New York: dover, 1967.

Geary, Kay. *A Course in Textile Design for the Weaver.* Parts 1, 2, and 3. McMinnville, Ore.: Kay Geary (distributed by Robin and Russ Handweavers), 1956.

Kurtz, Carol S. *Designing for Weaving: A Study Guide for Drafting, Designing, and Color.* Loveland, Colo.: Interweave Press, 1985.

National Bureau of Standards. *National Bureau of Standards Standard Reference Material Color Kit.* Washington, D.C.: U.S. Department of Commerce, 1976.

Periodicals

Handwoven. Interweave Press, 201 East Fourth Street, Loveland, Colo. 80537.

Prairie Wool Companion. 355 North Maine Avenue, Sioux Falls, S.D. 57102.

Shuttle Spindle & Dyepot. Handweavers Guild of America, 2402 University Avenue SE, Suite 702 , Saint Paul, Minn. 55114.

Weaver's Journal. P.O. Box 14-238, Saint Paul, Minn. 55114.

Manufacturers of rigid heddle looms

Ashford Handicrafts, Ltd., P.O. Box 474, Ashburton, New Zealand.

Beka, Inc., 542 Selby Avenue, Saint Paul, Minn. 55102.

Glimåkra USA, 50 Hall Lane, Clancy, M.T. 59634. (866) 890-7314. www.glimakraUSA.com.

Walter Kircher, Postfach 1608, 3550 Marburg/Lahn, West Germany.

Leclerc Corporation, 37 Elm Street, Champlain, N.Y. 12929.

Anders Lervad and Son A/S, Askov, 6600 Vejen, Denmark.

Nilus Leclerc, Inc., C.P. 69, L'Islet, Quebec, Canada G0R 2C0.

Schacht Spindle Company, Inc., 6101 Ben Place, Boulder, Colo. 80301.

GAV Glimåkra, Vavskedsvagen 2 Oxberg SE 792 94 Mora, Sweden. www.gavglimakra.se.

Warping Procedures
Quick Check

For threading back-to-front:

1. Determine size of project.

2. Calculate number of warp ends and length of warp; determine how much warp yarn is needed.

3. Measure warp on warping board, pegs, or other device.

4. Tie warp securely at the cross and with choke-ties.

5. Remove warp from warping board.

6. Place warp cross on hand. Place all fingers through the loop and the thumb between the tails of the warp chain. Move the ties at the cross down to the first choke-tie.

7. Lift the loops off the warp cross one at a time and thread them through the slots of the heddle. If you are using a loom which has plastic teeth on the beams, place each warp loop on a tooth which lines up with that loop's position in the heddle. If you are using a loom which has a dowel rod to which the warp will be fastened, slip the warp loops onto an extra dowel rod and fasten that rod into place.

8. Shake and smooth warp chain.

9. Wind warp onto back beam, using heavy paper to separate the layers.

10. Cut the end loops. Remove one strand from each slot and thread it through the hole next to it.

11. Lay warp ends in the appropriate teeth on the front beam or, if tying onto a dowel rod, gather warp ends into 1-inch groups. PLACE HEDDLE IN UP SHED POSITION on top of the shed blocks.

12. Tie the warp to the front beam alternating groups of warp ends from side to side toward the center.

13. Check tension for evenness; adjust if necessary.

14. READY TO WEAVE!

Summary of Projects

	Pages	Size of heddle	Minimum loom width	Techniques
Runner or pillow	14-15	8	14″ (35 cm)	Weft stripes and floats. Use of template.
Placemats	34-35	10	15″ (37.5 cm)*	Textured yarn in weft stripes.
Mohair shawl	38-39	12	20″ (50 cm)**	Warp stripes.
Weft-faced bags	46-47	10	13½″ (33.75 cm)	Weft-faced patterns, weft floats.
Leno runner	58-59	12	18″ (45 cm)***	Openwork.
Transparency inlay	64-65	10	18½″ (46.25 cm)*	Inlays.
Tapestry purse	70-71	10	8″ (20 cm)	Tapestry.
Easy tabard	74-75	8	20″ (50 cm)**	Color-and-weave effect.
Red vest	82-83	12	20″ (50 cm)**	Grouped warps and wefts.
Blue cotton top	100-101	12	14″ (35 cm)	Warp stripes.
Purple afghan	104-105	10	10″ (25 cm)	Weft stripes and floats.

To adapt projects for different HEDDLES, see the chart of yarns on page 13 for ideas. Remember that a heavier yarn produces a heavier fabric; this may work for the project you have in mind and it may not.

To adapt projects for different LOOM WIDTHS, various tactics are possible. Suggestions:

  * Simply make the piece narrower; scale down the drawing if necessary.

 ** Divide the project into two or three narrow panels which can be joined after they are woven.

*** Make the project narrower *or* redesign for panels.

Glossary

Balanced weave—A cloth structure in which there are as many wefts (picks) per inch as there are warps (ends) per inch; warp and weft are equally visible in the finished cloth.

Beam, cloth—The rotating piece of the loom located at the front, onto which the woven fabric is wound.

Beam, warp—The rotating piece of the loom located at the back, onto which the warp yarns are wound in preparation for weaving.

Beaming—The process of winding the warp onto the back beam of the loom.

Beat—To press the weft yarn in place with a rigid heddle, beater, batten, or sword. You can beat very firmly or very lightly, or anywhere in between, depending on the fabric you want to produce.

Bobbin—A plastic or wooden spool that holds yarn, for use with a boat shuttle. See also *quill*.

Bobbin winder—A geared device which winds yarn onto bobbins or paper quills to be used in a boat shuttle. An alternative is to fashion a slightly tapered dowel rod about 6 inches long and insert it in a variable-speed electric drill or food mixer.

Bubble—The technique of inserting the weft yarn in the shed in a series of curves or bubbles. It helps prevent draw-in, especially in weft-faced weaving.

Butterfly—A small bundle of yarn which can be used instead of a shuttle when you want to insert weft for a short distance, usually in tapestry or inlay work.

Crochet hook—Handy tool used to pull warp threads through the holes of the heddle and to tuck forgotten tails of weft back into the weaving. For threading, use a size 8 steel hook with 8-dent (32/10) and 10-dent (40/10) heddles, a size 10 hook for a 12-dent (48/10) heddle, or a size 13 hook for finer heddles.

Cross—The figure-eight that is made at one end of the warp while it is measured on the warping board, to keep the yarns in order. Also called *weaver's cross, warp cross*.

Dent—Refers to the spacing of a rigid heddle or a reed. For example, an 8-dent heddle can be threaded with 8 warp ends per inch if one end is placed in each hole or slot.

Dog—The part of the ratchet system that locks it. Also called a *pawl*.

Draw-in—The tendency of a fabric to get narrower as it is woven. A particular warp will tend to draw in by a specific amount. For example, a warp which you thread to a 10-inch (25 cm) width in the heddle may, when woven, produce a cloth which is consistently 9½ inches (22.5 cm) wide. Draw-in is a natural occurrence for which you can compensate. If you don't, (1) your weavings will be narrower than you intend, and (2) the outside warps will be under a great deal of stress during weaving and may break.

End—One warp thread.

EPI—Number of ends per inch.

Fell—The line made by the most recently inserted weft pick of the fabric being woven.

Finish—The technique(s) used to secure the warp ends on a completed piece of cloth so that the picks will stay in place.

Hand—The quality of a finished fabric, including softness or crispness, drapability or rigidity, and general feel.

Heddle—see *rigid heddle*.

Heddle holder, multi-heddle holder—A set of notched blocks used to hold the heddle upright during threading. On some looms a holder is incorporated with the shed blocks. The multi-heddle holder will hold two or three heddles upright; several heddles can be used together to increase the possible number of ends per inch or to allow more complex weaving structures. If you don't have special holders on your loom, attach a C-clamp to the bottom edge at one end of the extra heddle. The clamp provides a base to hold the heddle upright. A multi-heddle holder can be made easily from a scrap of $1 \times 2''$ lumber. Cut two or three notches about 6 inches (15 cm) apart on the narrow edge. Each notch should be ½ inch (1.25 cm) deep and as wide as the heddle is thick.

Inlay—A technique in which an additional or pattern yarn is inserted along with the background plain weave to form a design.

Loom waste—The portion of warp that cannot be woven; it consists of the amount used to tie the warp onto the cloth beam and weave the heading, and the amount that can't be woven behind the heddle(s), which secures the warp to the warp beam.

Pick—Weft row.

Pick-up stick—Flat wooden stick with one rounded end, used to pick up warp threads in some types of pattern weaving.

Plain weave—The basic weave structure of over-one/under-one. Sometimes also called *tabby*.

Ply—One strand of yarn; one of the strands twisted together to make a larger yarn. Also used to describe the size of yarn, in a rough way. Two strands spun together make a two-ply yarn. A finished yarn of only one ply (one strand) is referred to as a *singles*.

Quill—Simple alternative to the bobbins that store yarn for use in a boat shuttle. A quill can be made from a $3 \times 4''$ (7.5 × 10 cm) piece of brown paper by rolling it on the diagonal around a slender object like a pencil to produce a long, narrow tube.

Ratchet—The notched or toothed wheel on the end of a beam which is held in place by a pawl. The ratchet-and-pawl prevents the beam from turning and maintains tension on the warp. When more warp is needed, the pawl is released, the beam is rotated, and the warp is secured in its new position when the pawl is applied again at another point in the ratchet.

Rigid heddle—A frame containing plastic or metal bars, each of which has a hole in its center. The warp ends are threaded through the holes and through the slots between the bars. The rigid heddle raises and

117

lowers groups of warp ends and is used to beat the weft into place.

Rigid heddles most often come in 8-dent (32/10), 10-dent (40/10), and 12-dent (48/10). Usually only one heddle of one size is included with a loom. Two or three identical heddles can be used together to obtain more holes and slots per inch or for advanced rigid heddle weaving techniques.

Sample—A trial piece of weaving, used to check yarns, colors, and techniques.

Sampler—A weaving which shows a number of different techniques or variations.

Selvedge—The edge of the fabric where the weft turns to go back across the warp in the other direction.

Set—Verb for the spacing of warp ends. ''The warp is set at 10 EPI.''

Sett—Noun for the spacing of warp ends. ''The sett is 10 EPI.''

Shed—Opening between raised and lowered groups of warp ends, through which weft is passed.

Shot—Weft row; pick.

Shrinkage—Loss in length and width of finished weaving due to the relaxation of the yarns in the washing process.

Shuttles—Tools which store a quantity of weft and carry it through the sheds. Shuttles are most often made of wood and come in a variety of shapes and styles. *Stick shuttles* are flat wooden sticks, notched at both ends. These are the most inexpensive shuttles, and it's nice to have several in each of a variety of lengths on hand. When you are ready to weave, choose a stick shuttle which is slightly longer than your warp is wide. *Boat shuttles* are shaped somewhat like boats; they hold bobbins which have been wound with the weft yarn. The very thin Swedish boat shuttles can be used with a rigid heddle loom, and are especially nice for fine yarns. *Rag* or *rug shuttles* hold

more yarn than stick shuttles. They are especially useful for very heavy yarns or rag strips.

Skein—Yarn wound in a hank.

Take-up—The amount by which a warp is shortened during the weaving process; it depends on the weave structure and on the thickness and type of weft used. Weft-faced cloths experience less take-up than do warp-faced fabrics.

Tapestry—A predominantly plain weave and weft-faced technique where each weft color weaves back and forth in its own area to form a design, rather than weaving from selvedge to selvedge.

Template—A strip of paper or nonwoven interfacing fabric on which color changes or pattern sequences are marked so matching pieces can be woven.

Threading—The process of entering warp threads into the holes and slots of a rigid heddle or heddles; the specific sequence of positions into which warp threads are entered in the rigid heddle(s).

Umbrella swift—A frame that opens out like an umbrella and holds a skein of yarn taut so it can be unreeled and wound into a ball.

Warp—Lengthwise threads that are held under tension on the loom.

Warp cross—Also called *weaver's cross, cross.*

Warp-faced—Fabric in which the warp ends are spaced so closely together that the weft doesn't show.

Waste yarn—Scrap yarn used at the beginning and end of a weaving to hold the weft in place until the fabric is finished. Waste yarn is also used to spread the warp evenly at the beginning of the weaving.

Weaver's cross—Also called *cross, warp cross.*

Weft—Yarn woven crosswise through warp ends to make fabric.

Weft-faced—Fabric in which only the weft shows; the warp is spaced widely, so the weft slides down and covers it.

INDEX